# book of mormon

## big picture/little picture
# STUDY GUIDE

### by Cali Black
### creator of @comefollowmestudy

Created by Cali Black, Come Follow Me Study, LLC. This material is copyrighted. It is intended for use in one household. For additional permissions, contact Cali at caliblack@comefollowmestudy.com.

This material is neither made, provided, approved, nor endorsed by Intellectual Reserve, Inc. or The Church of Jesus Christ of Latter-day Saints. Any content or opinions expressed, implied or included in or with the material are solely those of the owner and not those of Intellectual Reserve, Inc. or The Church of Jesus Christ of Latter-day Saints.

# what to expect

## Hey! I am SO glad that you are here.

I love the scriptures, and I love feeling confident while I read. When I used to try to "study the scriptures", I would often feel confused, and I didn't really have a great experience. I felt like everyone else "got it", and I was stuck with a kid-level understanding.

I've spent years trying to learn about the background info for all of these intricate scripture stories. I've learned about people, symbolism, cultural differences, and facts galore.

But I also know that most people don't have time to read elaborate and detailed historical books in order to learn all of this for yourselves.

So I started creating study guides that were for people like me. Latter-day Saints who:
- **want to feel like they understand the scriptures more**
- **but don't have much extra time to devote to figuring it out**

As a former middle school teacher, I like to think I've mastered the art of simplification. I've taken countless hours of research and distilled them into what you REALLY need to know.

And then I realized that even more important than actually understanding what's going on in the scriptures, is figuring out how to <u>apply</u> them to my life and have them help to change me each day that I open their pages.

## And thus, my Big Picture/Little Picture Study Guides were born.

The perfect mix of content, short summaries, connections, and a whole bunch of spiritual focus. I think it's a pretty good recipe.

## If you've never used a Big Picture/Little Picture Study Guide, here's what to expect:

Each week, I give you EVERYTHING that you need to be successful on both ends of the scripture study spectrum: the background knowledge AND the spiritual application.

# BIG PICTURE

In the Big Picture section, I give you whatever historical, contextual, or interesting knowledge I think that you'll need to totally "get" what's going on. (In simple, bullet-point form, of course.)

# LITTLE PICTURE

After all that big context, we get to the nitty-gritty daily reading part.

I give a quick little reference for every single chapter that we read, including a couple of sentences about what you should know/remember BEFORE you read, and then a simple summary of WHAT you are reading in that chapter. (Just in case things get confusing!)

# SPIRITUAL GUIDING QUESTIONS

This is, of course, where the rubber meets the road in WHY we study the scriptures. I've created 7 questions for you to ponder each week, so you could respond to one each day, do them all at once, or pick and choose which questions resonate with you.

**Pretty much, I've packed as much info into this little study guide as I could while still keeping a conversational feel, because talking about the scriptures is super fun.**

If you've been wanting to feel "in the know" before Sunday School lessons, if you've been looking for an easier way to understand the scriptures in order to teach your kids, if you've been looking to boost your knowledge before YOU stand up and teach seminary, then I believe this study guide is exactly what you need.

**Above all though, never let this study guide, or anything else for that matter, separate you from getting in the actual scriptures. In fact, I hope this guide encourages you to get in the scriptures more often. Nothing is more important than you, with the Spirit, reading the word of God!**

I am so excited to help orient you in the Book of Mormon this year. This first quarter, studying the words of Nephi, is filled with some amazing Old Testament connections and beautiful doctrine centered on Jesus Christ.

For ease, this study guide has been broken into quarters for the year. Future study guides for April-June, July-September, and October-December will be available on Amazon or through comefollowmestudy.com in a timely manner as we move through the year.

I love connecting with people and talking about the scriptures, so make sure you follow me on Instagram @comefollowmestudy, on Facebook.com/comefollowmestudy, or join my email list at comefollowmestudy.com. I also co-host the One Minute Scripture Study podcast wherever you listen to podcasts!

**Alright, are you feeling ready?! Let's go! Happy Studying!**

**- Cali Black**

# cool features

## For each week this quarter, you'll find:

**General Context:** These bullet points remind your brain what we studied the week before, and give you any context you need for the current reading in order to connect the story together.

**Spiritual Themes:** Sometimes there is so much stuff in a reading assignment that it's hard to know where to focus! That's why you'll get three spiritual themes each week to help you focus on some of the most important topics. These would be great to highlight or note in your scriptures as you actually study, or you can just keep them in mind to guide you as you read through the assigned chapters!

**People to Know:** This is a quick bullet point list that includes descriptions and extra info about people. Anyone that is mentioned in that week's reading gets put on the list so that you always have an easy reference, especially if you need to jog your memory on who they are.

**Places to Know:** This bullet point list gives a quick rundown of all the locations mentioned in that week's reading. Having a good grasp on where stories are taking place, and who is from where, can make a huge difference in understanding these scriptures.

**Chapter Breakdowns:** Often, we aren't sitting down to read the entire week's chapters in one sitting. So if you read all the general context, feel like you totally "get it", and then read one chapter. . . When you sit down to read the next day, it may have all disappeared from your brain. That's why I give you a "BEFORE YOU READ" quick reminder before every single chapter. I also give a "WHAT YOU'LL READ" with a chapter summary in case you want to double check you understood what you just read.

**Spiritual Guiding Questions:** This is where you get to put your own pencil to the paper and practice applying the scriptures. There are seven questions for each week, so you could ponder one each day, do them all at one time, or only focus on the questions that resonate with you. These also make great discussion questions if you are a teacher!

# book of mormon map

**What starts out as simply "the promised land" quickly turns into a complex civilization filled with lands, cities, and borders.**

It always helps my brain to be able to keep track of locations if I can actually see them on a map.

Unfortunately, we don't have an accurate historic map of every location in the Book of Mormon.

**But do you know what we do have?! The amazing Sarah Cook from Olivet Designs. She went through the entire Book of Mormon, tracked every location and their relation to each other or natural features, and created a fantastic Book of Mormon map!**

You are going to want to turn back to this map over and over again as we study the Book of Mormon so you can better picture in your mind what it might have looked like to travel from one city or land to another.

**And I want to add the disclaimer that this map is simply an artistic interpretation of the cities and landforms we read about. It is not meant to be compared to actual geographic locations, nor can we even come close to accuracy in distance.**

**Again, a huge thank you to Sarah Cook from Olivet Designs for allowing me to share this super useful map with you this year.**

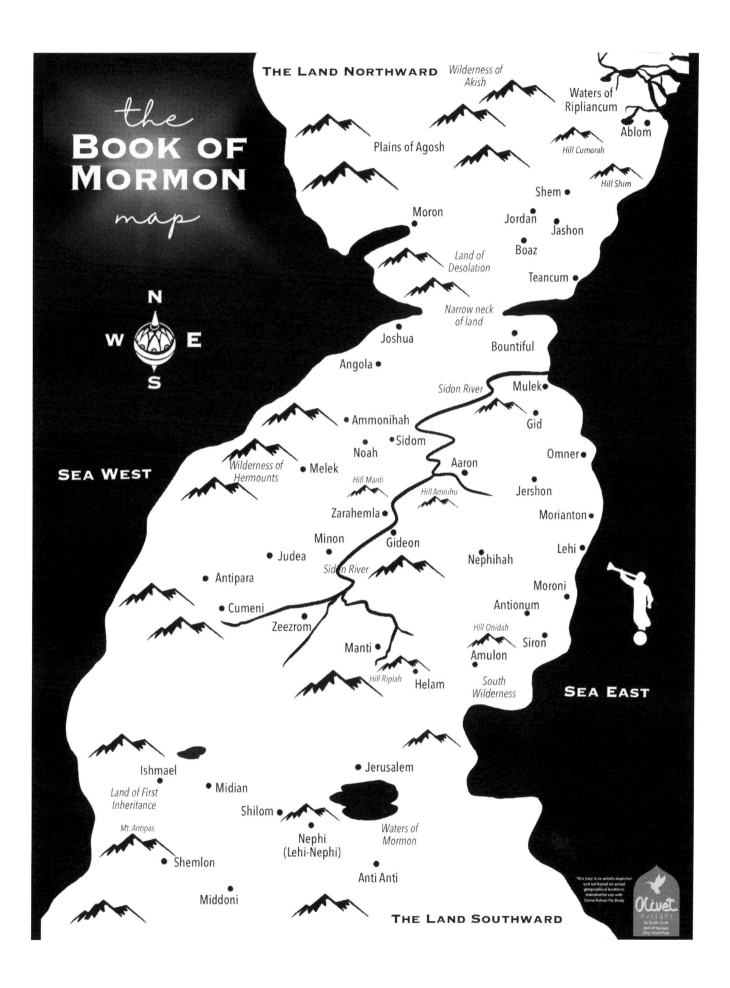

# INTRODUCTORY PAGES OF THE BOOK OF MORMON

## *"Another Testament of Jesus Christ"*

# BIG PICTURE

*How to feel confident fitting in this week's readings with the entire Book of Mormon*

## General Context:

- **The introductory pages of the Book of Mormon are often, let's be honest, pages we skip over in our personal studies.** But this week will serve as a beautiful introductory period to "set the scene" and remind us of the sacrifices that were made in many dispensations to bring us this ancient record.
- **The 6 distinct portions in the introductory pages can be split into 3 different time periods** for when they were written:
  - Ancient Book of Mormon time period: **The Title Page**
  - Restoration time period: **The Testimony of Three Witnesses, The Testimony of the Eight Witnesses, The Testimony of Joseph Smith**
  - Modern time period: **The Introduction, The Brief Explanation**
- **The Title Page to the Book of Mormon is the only part of these introductory pages that was actually on the gold plates!** Skipping forward to the very end of the Book of Mormon, you may remember that Moroni was the one who buried all the plates in the hill. His father, Mormon, had compiled the records, but Moroni was tasked with adding his own thoughts after his father was killed. Moroni wrote what we now call "The Title Page of the Book of Mormon", explaining where the records came from and the purpose for why God preserved the records. As you read Moroni's short message, try to picture him all alone, as the final righteous person left in the land, writing to a people that he trusted would someday read what he, his father, and countless others had sacrificed so much to preserve.

- **The three "testimony" documents in the introductory pages are from the 1800s**- the Testimonies of the Three Witnesses, of the Eight Witnesses, and of Joseph Smith. The testimonies from both the three witnesses and the eight witnesses were given only a month apart in June and July of 1829. From the time that Joseph Smith received the gold plates in 1827, he had been the only person who had officially seen them. In 1829, Joseph was given permission to show the plates first to three witnesses: Oliver Cowdery, David Whitmer, and Martin Harris. A month later, even more were given permission to view the plates. Each group wrote a testimony and signed their names to it. **"The Testimony of Joseph Smith" was written by Joseph Smith himself in 1838, and is an excerpt from Joseph Smith-History.** This excerpt tells the story of how Joseph Smith first learned about the plates from the Angel Moroni, how he visited Hill Cumorah each year for 4 years in preparation, and how Joseph ultimately retrieved the plates. As you read these three documents from the 1800s, think about all of the miracles and all of the sacrifices that were necessary to bring the Book of Mormon forward in a way that future Saints could trust.
- **Both the Introduction and the Brief Explanation are modern additions from the church in 1981.** The Introduction is meant to give anyone reading through this book for the first time a quick summary of where the records came from, what events they cover, how Joseph Smith obtained them, and the spiritual blessings that are promised to those who study the book. The Brief Explanation is SUPER HELPFUL and you will probably want to refer to it as we study the entire Book of Mormon this year. It describes the 4 different sources for the plates in the Book of Mormon, as well as the order of the books. You'll also find a good reminder of which parts we see in our current scriptures that are original to the plates, and which parts are added for our convenience.

# Spiritual Themes:

Look for these themes as you read the chapters this week! Find examples in the scriptures, and ponder on what these themes can look like in your life.

- **The purpose of the Book of Mormon**

- **The power of witnesses**

- **God's hand in the coming forth of the Book of Mormon**

# People to Know:

- **Joseph Smith**
  - Joseph Smith's First Vision in 1820 started the process of the restoration of the fullness of the gospel of Jesus Christ. But before the church could be formed in 1830, there was something absolutely essential that was missing: the Book of Mormon. On the night of September 21, 1823, the Angel Moroni appeared to Joseph Smith in his bedroom. Moroni taught young Joseph about the records of his people and where he could find them. Moroni repeated the message 3 more times over the next day until Joseph told his dad about the vision. Joseph found the hill and the rock where the plates were buried, but Moroni told him it wasn't time to get them yet. For the next 4 years, Joseph met with Moroni at the hill on the same day. Finally, in 1827, Joseph was given permission to take the plates home to begin the translation process. In 1828, all of the translation done up to that point was lost when Joseph let Martin Harris take the transcripts. Almost all of the Book of Mormon that we have now was translated between April and June of 1829. The Book of Mormon was then ready to be published right before the church was officially formed in April of 1830.

- **Moroni**
  - Moroni was the final righteous person left at the end of the Book of Mormon. He spent years hidden, all alone, adding to the records that his father had compiled. He finished the book "Mormon" after his father died, abridged and wrote the book of "Ether" about the Jaredites, and then wrote the book of "Moroni". He buried all of the records in a hill. In 1823, the now resurrected Angel Moroni appeared to Joseph Smith and told him all about the records. Moroni met with Joseph at the nearby Hill Cumorah each year for the next 4 years, preparing and teaching Joseph. In 1827, Moroni told Joseph that he could take the plates to his home to begin the translation process. Joseph later said that once the translation process was done, he returned the plates back to Moroni.

- **Mormon**
  - He earned the name of the entire compilation of the ancient records that we have, and rightfully so! At the age of 10, Mormon was told that in the future he would find the ancient records that Ammaron hid in a hill. After seeing Jesus Christ at age 15, and becoming a military captain at age 16, Mormon led the Nephites during a time where they were turning away from the truth. He found the plates of Nephi when he was 24, and spent much of his life reading and then abridging, or rewriting in a shorter or more succinct way, the books of Mosiah, Alma, Helaman, 3 Nephi, and 4 Nephi. He wrote more than this, presumably including the book of Lehi, that Martin Harris lost the transcripts for. Mormon also wrote Words of Mormon and most of Mormon before passing the record to his son Moroni prior to his death.

# Where are We?

- **Hill Cumorah**
  - This is the hill in modern-day upstate New York where Moroni buried the plates that became the Book of Mormon. Hundreds of years later, this is where Joseph Smith was led by a now resurrected Angel Moroni to retrieve the gold plates and eventually translate them.

# LITTLE PICTURE

*How to understand each chapter and apply principles to my life*

- **Title Page of the Book of Mormon:**
  - **Before You Read:** This Title Page is written by Moroni, the one who buried the plates anciently. This is skipping ALL the way to the end of the Book of Mormon (spoiler alert), but remember that Moroni is writing this with a full record abridged by his father Mormon, and having seen the destruction of all of his people. He writes this title page and gives his purpose for hiding the plates away.
  - **What You'll Read About:** Moroni explains that this book is an abridgement of records written to Lamanites, Jews, and Gentiles and hidden to be brought forth someday. He writes the purposes for these records, including convincing all that Jesus is the Christ.

- **Introduction:**
  - **Before You Read:** This introduction is not original to the Book of Mormon. It was added by the modern church in 1981.
  - **What You'll Read About:** The Book of Mormon is a book of scripture written by many ancient prophets who lived in the Americas around 600 BC - 400 AD. The records were buried in a hill until Joseph Smith found and translated them by the power of God. All are invited to read the Book of Mormon and ask God for a witness of its truth.

- **The Testimony of the Three Witnesses:**
  - **Before You Read:** Until June 1829 when Joseph was allowed to show three men the original plates of the Book of Mormon, he had been the sole official witness to their reality. The men chosen as witnesses, Oliver Cowdery, Martin Harris, and David Whitmer, had all contributed to the coming forth of the Book of Mormon in some way.
  - **What You'll Read About:** Oliver Cowdery, David Whitmer, and Martin Harris testify that they have seen the plates of the Book of Mormon brought down by an angel. They testify that the translation is true and that they have been commanded to be witnesses.

- **The Testimony of the Eight Witnesses:**
  - **Before You Read:** Shortly after Joseph showed the plates to the three witnesses, Joseph was authorized by God to show the gold plates to eight more witnesses in July 1829.
  - **What You'll Read About:** The eight witnesses testify that they physically saw and handled the gold plates. They describe the appearance of the pages and engravings on them.

- **The Testimony of the Prophet Joseph Smith:**
  - **Before You Read:** This testimony is an excerpt from Joseph Smith-History in the Pearl of Great Price, and outlines Joseph Smith's story learning about and finally obtaining the plates he translated to the Book of Mormon.
  - **What You'll Read About:** Joseph Smith tells the story of the Angel Moroni appearing to him in his bedroom in 1823 to tell him about the buried gold plates and Urim and Thummim. The messenger instructs Joseph to tell his father, and Joseph finds where the plates are buried. He is not allowed to take the box with the plates for another four years until he is ready. He faces immense persecution and opposition once he has the plates.

- **A Brief Explanation About the Book of Mormon:**
  - **Before You Read:** This page is a modern addition to the Book of Mormon to explain the main portions of the book and any important features a reader should understand.
  - **What You'll Read About:** First, this explanation outlines the four sources that make up the Book of Mormon. Then, it explains the organization of the books, including identifying which books are abridged by Mormon. Finally, it outlines how to know if something is original to the text, or added by the church as a helpful feature.

# SPIRITUAL GUIDING QUESTIONS

Question: What do you learn about the purpose of the Book of Mormon through the Title Page? (Title Page)

Question: Why is it so important to know the great things that the Lord did for our ancestors, both recent and ancient? (Title Page)

Question: What is the most important event in the Book of Mormon? Why do we need to know about this? (Introduction)

Question: What have you experienced in your life to agree with Joseph saying, "a man would get nearer to God by abiding by its precepts, than by any other book"? (Introduction)

Question: If you were asked to write your own witness of the Book of Mormon to be included with the other witnesses, what would you say? (The Testimony of the Three Witnesses)

Question: Why do you think the Angel Moroni repeated the same message four times to the teenage Joseph Smith? What does that tell you about how God teaches us?
(The Testimony of Joseph Smith)

Question: What can you learn from how Joseph's father responded to learning about Joseph's visitations from the Angel Moroni? (The Testimony of Joseph Smith)

# 1 NEPHI 1-5

### *"I Will Go and Do"*

# BIG PICTURE

*How to feel confident fitting in this week's readings with the entire New Testament*

## General Context:

- **Let's jump into the first book in the Book of Mormon: 1 Nephi! The book that everyone has read a million times.** One of the cool advantages to studying a book that you probably know pretty well is that it leaves more space to focus on the spiritual lessons. Even the spiritual lessons that are repeated often (like "go and do" or "born of goodly parents") can take on a new life as we read and ponder on them again. Since we are different each time we read and ponder, the Spirit can give us the personalized messages we need if we humble ourselves and look for where we see ourselves in the story.

- **Who wrote 1 Nephi?** No trick questions here! Nephi wrote all of the First Book of Nephi. You'll notice this entire book is written from the 1st person point of view (meaning he uses the pronouns "I", "my", "we"...). **It is interesting to remember that Nephi wrote this account as a much older prophet-leader in the promised land.** He wasn't writing this account like a journal while the events were happening. This means that he has perspective on his side when he writes these stories, so look for his editorial narration. He can see the bigger picture and even mentions in chapter 6 that he is only including things that will "persuade men to come unto God".

- **What was going on when the events in 1 Nephi began?** Ready to take a quick trip back to Old Testament times? It is around the year 600 B.C.
  - In the Old Testament, we learn that the children of Israel split themselves into two kingdoms: Israel in the north and Judah in the south. The tribe of Manasseh was part of the northern kingdom.
  - In 2 Kings 17, we learn that the northern kingdom of Israel fell to the Assyrians and Israel was scattered. Some Israelites from the northern kingdom escaped to the southern kingdom of Judah. This would have been Lehi's ancestors, since he belonged to the tribe of Manasseh. These scattered Israelites took refuge in Judah, in the capital city of Jerusalem, until the kingdom of Judah was conquered by the Babylonians, completing the full scattering of all the tribes of Israel.

- In 2 Kings 24-25, we learn about king Zedekiah, who ruled right before the second big attack from the Babylonians on Jerusalem. We know that Lehi and his family were able to escape Jerusalem before it fell to the Babylonians.
- **So to sum it up:** The children of Israel had been growing in wickedness and turning away from God, and it was time for them to be "scattered" (which means they were conquered and taken away to various places). Many Israelites had already been scattered, but Jerusalem had been a stronghold. Lehi and his family were here in Jerusalem when the vision came telling them to leave before Jerusalem would be completely conquered and carried into Babylon.

# Spiritual Themes:

Look for these themes as you read the chapters this week! Find examples in the scriptures, and ponder on what these themes can look like in your life.

- **Willingness to act**

- **The importance of the scriptures**

- **Being led by God's hand**

# People to Know:

- **Lehi:**
  - Lehi was a prophet who lived a relatively comfortable life in Jerusalem. He was married to Sariah, and he followed God's commandment to take his family into the wilderness to flee the impending destruction of Jerusalem by the Babylonians. Lehi then received a vision that told him to send his sons back to Jerusalem to get the records from Laban. Once his sons were back with the records, Lehi searched the scriptures joyfully.
- **Sariah:**
  - Sariah was the matriarch of the family and Lehi's wife. She supported her husband, complained against him when she believed her sons were lost, and felt a strong confirmation of her husband's prophetic calling when they returned safely.
- **Nephi:**
  - Nephi was the youngest son of Lehi and Sariah at the time they left Jerusalem. He was obedient to the Lord and to his father. He willingly traveled back to Jerusalem with his brothers to get the brass plates and insisted they not give up even after failure. He eventually returned with the brass plates back to his parents in the wilderness.

- **Laman:**
  - Laman was Nephi's oldest brother. In these chapters, we learn that he usually (although sometimes begrudgingly) listened to his father, but he generally had a hard time believing in God's hand in many of the events. Laman was the first to try to get the brass plates from Laban, but he was chased away.
- **Lemuel:**
  - Lemuel was another one of Nephi's older brothers, and generally followed Laman's lead.
- **Sam:**
  - Sam was Nephi's older brother. Sam was more humble and willing to follow Lehi and Nephi with faith.
- **Laban:**
  - Laban was a powerful man who had the record of the Jews at his residence in Jerusalem, including genealogy and their scriptures.
- **Zoram:**
  - Zoram was Laban's servant who ended up going with Nephi's family after helping them obtain the records of the Jews.

# Where are We?

- **Jerusalem**
  - Jerusalem had already suffered an attack from the Babylonians, but had grown proud, believing they could never actually be conquered. We know from the Old Testament that the Lord called many prophets in Jerusalem at this time, yet the majority of the people turned away from God. After Lehi and his family left, Jerusalem was conquered and many of the inhabitants were taken away to Babylon.
- **Wilderness near the Red Sea**
  - Lehi and Sariah's family start their journey into the wilderness.

# LITTLE PICTURE

*How to understand each chapter and apply principles to my life*

- **1 Nephi 1:**
  - **Before You Read:** Nephi, a righteous Jewish man of God, is writing about his family's history living in wicked Jerusalem and eventually crossing the ocean to the Americas. The record starts around 600 BC.
  - **What You'll Read About:** Nephi introduces himself and explains that he will make a true record of his life. Lehi, Nephi's father, is a prophet in Jerusalem and sees a vision of God the Father, Jesus Christ, and angels. He learns in the vision that Jerusalem will be destroyed because of its wickedness. Lehi tries to preach to the people in Jerusalem, but they get very angry. Nephi explains that he will make an abridgement of his father's records of his visions and hopes to show God's mercy through this record.

- **1 Nephi 2:**
  - **Before You Read:** In the previous chapter, Nephi's father Lehi saw a vision warning him that Jerusalem would be destroyed because of wickedness.
  - **What You'll Read About:** God commands Lehi in a dream to leave Jerusalem, so he takes his family (Sariah, Laman, Lemuel, Sam, and Nephi), provisions, and tents into the wilderness. They pitch their tents in a valley Lehi calls Lemuel, next to a river he calls Laman. Laman and Lemuel murmur against their father, but Nephi prays to God and receives a witness that his father is leading them in doing the right thing. Nephi receives a promise from God that he will be blessed and be made a ruler over his brothers because of his righteousness.

- **1 Nephi 3:**
  - **Before You Read:** In the last chapter, Lehi and his family journeyed into the wilderness to escape the coming destruction of Jerusalem. Nephi humbled himself, while Laman and Lemuel murmured.
  - **What You'll Read About:** Lehi has a dream commanding Nephi and his brothers to return to Jerusalem to retrieve brass plates containing scriptures and genealogy from a man named Laban. Lehi's sons return to Jerusalem and attempt to obtain the plates. First, Laman simply asks for them. Then they try to buy the plates using the riches they left in their home. They are unsuccessful and almost get killed, so Laman and Lemuel complain and beat their younger brothers. An angel appears to them and instructs them to stop and try obtaining the plates again, promising that the Lord will deliver Laban into their hands.

- **1 Nephi 4:**
  - **Before You Read:** So far, Laman, Lemuel, Sam, and Nephi have been unsuccessful in obtaining the brass plates from Laban, but an angel just came and promised that Laban would be delivered into their hands.
  - **What You'll Read About:** Nephi has faith and heads back towards the house of Laban. The Spirit leads Nephi to find Laban drunk and passed out on the ground, and Nephi is constrained by the Lord to kill Laban with his own sword. He obeys the Lord's commandment, and dresses in Laban's clothes. Nephi pretends to be Laban and has a servant go get the brass plates. He and the servant, Zoram, bring the plates to Nephi's brothers outside the city walls. Zoram agrees to go with the brothers and they return to their father, Lehi.

- **1 Nephi 5:**
  - **Before You Read:** In the last chapter, Nephi obtained the brass plates, and he returned with his brothers and Zoram back to Lehi.
  - **What You'll Read About:** In the wilderness, Sariah complains against Lehi and Lehi comforts her. They all rejoice when they are reunited, and Sariah praises the Lord. Lehi searches the brass plates and finds many books of scripture and a genealogy of his fathers. Lehi prophesies about his descendants and the plates of brass.

# SPIRITUAL GUIDING QUESTIONS

Question: One of the first things Nephi wrote about was his father's vision. Why do you think it's significant that he chose to include a heavenly vision within the first few verses of this book?
(1 Nephi 1:6-15)

Question: What is a "tender mercy" you have experienced recently? How could you get better at recognizing tender mercies in your life? (1 Nephi 1:20)

Question: Which characteristics of Nephi and Sam helped them turn to the Lord when Laman and Lemuel choose to murmur? (1 Nephi 2:16-19)

Question: What is a commandment that is difficult for you to fully embody right now? How can Nephi's teachings give you confidence? (1 Nephi 3:7)

Question: Why do you think the brothers failed twice before being successful in getting the brass plates when God was the one who commanded them to go there in the first place? What could you learn from this? (1 Nephi 3:11-27)

Question: How might you react to being in Sariah's situation? What can you learn from her testimony? (1 Nephi 5:8)

Question: Why was it important that they have the brass plates? How does this make you feel about the importance of our scriptures today? (1 Nephi 5:14-22)

# 1 NEPHI 6 - 10

## *"Come and Partake of the Fruit"*

# BIG PICTURE

*How to feel confident fitting in this week's readings with the entire New Testament*

## General Context:

- **Lehi's family has been reunited all together with the important brass plates.** They are ready to travel more in the wilderness toward this "promised land". But wait, the Lord is going to ask them to head back to Jerusalem one more time! This week, we'll read about why Nephi and his brothers return to Jerusalem again, and we'll also hear Lehi tell his children about his vision of the Tree of Life.

- **Chapters 6 and 9 are unique because we get some glimpses into Nephi's future!** Nephi is writing this record years after the events actually happened. So picture Nephi, already married, already successfully living in the promised land, and already creating a new society with the family members who have stayed faithful to the Lord. Nephi shares that he is writing this record "to persuade men to come unto God". As you read, think about why these events and details were memorable decades later, and why he felt they would fulfill his purpose of bringing others closer to God. In fact, we are the literal audience Nephi was writing his records for, so how did he do? Have his writings brought you closer to God?

- **We will read about the vision of the Tree of Life twice:** This week, we get Lehi's version of the vision that he tells to his sons. Next week, we'll learn what Nephi experienced when he asked the Lord to see the vision for himself.

- **When are these events happening?** It's around 600 B.C.

# Spiritual Themes:

Look for these themes as you read the chapters this week! Find examples in the scriptures, and ponder on what these themes can look like in your life.

- **God's hand in saving the righteous**

- **Inviting others to experience God's goodness**

- **God will reveal secrets to those who ask Him**

# People to Know:

- **Nephi:**
  - Nephi was the youngest son of Lehi and Sariah at the time they left Jerusalem. He was obedient to the Lord and to his father. He willingly traveled back to Jerusalem two separate times, to retrieve both the brass plates and Ishmael's family.
- **Lehi:**
  - Lehi was a prophet who lived a relatively comfortable life in Jerusalem and then followed God's commandment to take his family into the wilderness to flee the impending destruction of Jerusalem by the Babylonians. In these chapters, he sees an important vision of the Tree of Life and shares it with his family.
- **Sariah:**
  - Sariah was the matriarch of the family and Lehi's wife. She supported her husband and had strong faith.
- **Laman:**
  - Laman was Nephi's oldest brother. He generally begrudgingly listened to his father, but he had a hard time believing in God's hand in many of the events.
- **Lemuel:**
  - Lemuel was another one of Nephi's older brothers, and generally followed Laman's lead.
- **Sam:**
  - Sam was Nephi's older brother. Sam was more humble and willing to follow Lehi and Nephi with faith.

- **Ishmael:**
  - Ishmael was a resident in Jerusalem who ended up going with Lehi's family into the wilderness. Ishmael's family included his wife, their 5 daughters, and their 2 sons. Some of the daughters married the children of Lehi, including Nephi.

# Where are We?

- **Jerusalem**
  - For the final time, we are in Jerusalem this week. Nephi and his brothers return from the wilderness once more in order to persuade Ishmael to join them on their journey. Shortly afterward, Jerusalem would be conquered by the Babylonians.
- **Wilderness near the Red Sea**
  - The wilderness where Lehi and Sariah stay is located south of Jerusalem in a valley that Lehi named "Lemuel". Nephi and his brothers arrive back in this valley with Ishmael and his family.

# LITTLE PICTURE

*How to understand each chapter and apply principles to my life*

- **1 Nephi 6:**
  - **Before You Read:** This super short chapter is unique because we get a break in the normal narration. Nephi gets personal, and tells us how he is choosing which things to record and not record on the plates. Remember, he is actually writing all this account later in his life in the promised land, so this is him explaining his criteria.
  - **What You'll Read About:** Nephi writes that many details about their genealogy and history will be in his father's record, but here he will write things to persuade men to come unto God.

- **1 Nephi 7:**
  - **Before You Read:** In 1 Nephi 5, Lehi's sons had just returned with the brass plates and Lehi bore testimony of their importance.
  - **What You'll Read About:** Lehi receives revelation that their family should not be alone, so Nephi and his brothers return again to Jerusalem. They convince Ishmael and his family to come to the wilderness with them so that the brothers can marry and have children. Ishmael agrees and departs into the wilderness with his wife, 5 daughters, and 2 sons. Some of them rebel on the journey and Nephi reminds Laman and Lemuel that the Lord is saving them and has already saved them from so much. Laman and Lemuel bind Nephi and want to leave him to die, but Nephi is able to break the binds through God's power, forgives his brothers, and they finish their journey to their father Lehi.

- **1 Nephi 8:**
  - **Before You Read:** In the last chapter, Nephi and his brothers brought Ishmael and his family to join them in the wilderness.
  - **What You'll Read About:** Lehi explains that he saw a vision in which he was led to a dark and dreary area. He found a field with the Tree of Life, whose fruit brought great joy. He invited the rest of his family to eat the fruit, but Laman and Lemuel would not come. He saw people moving along an iron rod toward the tree, but many got lost along the way. Lehi saw a great and spacious building full of people mocking those on the iron rod. He also saw others pressing forward on the iron rod who made it to the tree and ate the fruit.

- **1 Nephi 9:**
  - **Before You Read:** Once again, we get a small break in the narration from "current Nephi" as he is writing this record later in life.
  - **What You'll Read About:** Nephi explains that he wrote two records: the large plates of Nephi (containing more of the history) and the small plates (containing the spiritual things). What we are reading is the small plates.

- **1 Nephi 10:**
  - **Before You Read:** Lehi just finished telling his family all about his vision of the Tree of Life. Remember the group in the wilderness now includes both Lehi's and Ishmael's families.
  - **What You'll Read About:** Nephi writes about the beautiful testimony Lehi gives of the coming of the Savior 600 years in the future. Lehi teaches about a prophet (John the Baptist) who would prepare the way for the Savior. Lehi prophesies about the scattering of Israel, comparing Israel to an olive tree. Nephi then writes that those who diligently seek truth will find it through the Holy Ghost.

# SPIRITUAL GUIDING QUESTIONS

Question: Why was Ishmael's family needed, and why do you think this happened on a separate journey than retrieving the brass plates? (1 Nephi 7:1-5)

Question: Why was it so dangerous that Laman and Lemuel kept "forgetting" what the Lord had done for them already? How can you do better at remembering spiritual experiences you've already had? (1 Nephi 7:10-12)

Question: When Nephi's brothers were so angry with him, who was able to finally soften their hearts? Who is someone who needs help that you could advocate for? (1 Nephi 7:19)

Question: When have you forgiven someone that was difficult for you to forgive? Why do you think we are asked to forgive everyone? (1 Nephi 7:21)

Question: Why do you think Lehi wandered for so long in darkness before the full vision began? What could this mean or symbolize? (1 Nephi 8:7-9)

Question: What is a prompting you followed in your past that clearly led to a meaningful event? What is a prompting you've been currently ignoring, confused by, or putting off that you could follow with faith? (1 Nephi 9:5)

Question: What stands out to you from Lehi's beautiful testimony of Christ? (1 Nephi 10:4-6)

# 1 NEPHI 11 - 15

## "Armed with Righteousness and with the Power of God"

# BIG PICTURE

*How to feel confident fitting in this week's readings with the entire New Testament*

## General Context:

- **Ready for another vision?** Last week, we studied Lehi's vision of the Tree of Life that he shared with his sons. All of his sons were clearly intrigued and confused by what their father told them. In the chapters this week, we will see what the other brothers chose to do, and we will see what Nephi chose to do, which is to ask the Lord to see what his father had seen.
  - **In chapters 11-14,** Nephi will describe in detail the vision that he saw.
  - **In chapter 15**, we will learn what his brothers did and how they interacted with Nephi following his vision.
- **Look for differences between Lehi's vision and Nephi's vision.** There will clearly be some differences because Nephi gets to share his own perspective of his vision, while he can only describe what his father said about his vision. But notice how Nephi specifically is asking for the interpretation of the items in the vision of the tree of life. And in response, the Spirit of the Lord and an angel show him all about Jesus Christ and the future of the world.
- **There are some fun Old and New Testament connections in Nephi's vision!** Look for his descriptions of the Abrahamic covenant, Jesus' birth and life, the 12 apostles spreading the gospel, and John's vision contained in the Book of Revelation.
- **Who wrote it?** It's Nephi! Nephi wrote this account of his own experiences years after the actual events occurred.
- **And when is it?** It is around the year 600 B.C. Jerusalem still stands, although we know it will fall to the Babylonians soon.

# Spiritual Themes:

Look for these themes as you read the chapters this week! Find examples in the scriptures, and ponder on what these themes can look like in your life.

- **Asking God for your own answers**

- **The importance of the Book of Mormon**

- **The covenant between God and the House of Israel**

# People to Know:

- **Nephi:**
  - Nephi was the youngest son of Lehi and Sariah at the time they left Jerusalem. He was obedient to the Lord and to his father. After hearing his father's vision of the Tree of Life, Nephi asks to see the vision for himself, and he is blessed with a lengthy vision of the history of the world.
- **Lehi:**
  - Lehi was a prophet who lived a relatively comfortable life in Jerusalem and then followed God's commandment to take his family into the wilderness to flee the impending destruction of Jerusalem by the Babylonians. In the previous chapters, Lehi had shared a vision of the Tree of Life that he had seen with his sons.
- **Laman:**
  - Laman was Nephi's oldest brother. He generally begrudgingly listened to his father, but he had a hard time believing in God's hand in many of the events.
- **Lemuel:**
  - Lemuel was another one of Nephi's older brothers, and generally followed Laman's lead.
- **Sam:**
  - Sam was Nephi's older brother. Sam was more humble and willing to follow Lehi and Nephi with faith.

# Where are We?

- **The Wilderness near the Red Sea**
  - Lehi's family, Ishmael's family, and Zoram are all in the wilderness in the Valley of Lemuel.

# LITTLE PICTURE

*How to understand each chapter and apply principles to my life*

- **1 Nephi 11:**
  - **Before You Read:** In the last few chapters, Nephi described his father's vision of the Tree of Life, and some of Lehi's teachings to his family following that dream.
  - **What You'll Read About:** Nephi prays to see the vision his father saw and is carried away by the Spirit. Nephi sees the same beautiful tree his father saw, and asks the Spirit to know the interpretation of the vision. He sees the virgin Mary have a son, Jesus Christ. He learns the tree represents the love of God, and the iron rod is the word of God. Nephi witnesses Christ be baptized and minister among the Jews. He sees the crucifixion of Christ. Many gather in the great and spacious building to fight against the Lamb and His twelve apostles, but the wicked are ultimately destroyed.

- **1 Nephi 12:**
  - **Before You Read:** Nephi has been describing his own vision of the Tree of Life and the interpretation he is discovering.
  - **What You'll Read About:** Nephi's vision now turns to what will happen in the promised land. He describes wars and destruction among his own people, followed by the Lamb of God appearing to them. Christ chooses 12 disciples among Nephi's seed. He witnesses the Nephites and Lamanites fighting each other. The angel explains more symbols from Lehi's dream, and Nephi witnesses his descendants being defeated by the Lamanites and becoming wicked.

- **1 Nephi 13:**
  - **Before You Read:** In the previous chapter, Nephi described his vision of the wars and destruction between the Nephites and Lamanites. He continues describing his vision in the coming chapter.
  - **What You'll Read About:** Nephi sees a great church form among the many nations of the Gentiles. The head of the church is the devil, and it persecutes the saints. Nephi describes the colonization of the Americas. He sees the Bible go forth among the Gentiles, and lose many of its plain and precious parts. He sees that the Gentiles in the Americas will prosper, and that the remnant of the Lamanites will not be completely destroyed. God will then bring forth the restoration of plain and precious truths, and the Bible and other books will go from the Gentiles to the remnant of the Lamanites. The Lamb will be the One God over all the world.

- **1 Nephi 14:**
  - **Before You Read:** Nephi has been describing his own vision of the future of his people, along with interpretations of his father's vision of the Tree of Life.
  - **What You'll Read About:** Nephi talks about the blessings that will come upon the Gentiles who accept the Lamb in the last days. He also talks about the cursing that awaits those who are part of the great and abominable church. The great and abominable church has great power and authority in the world and gathers together against the church of the Lamb, who are few in number. The Saints will have the power of God. Nephi sees that the apostle John will write about the end of the world, and that John is the only one authorized to do so. Nephi ends his description of the vision, stating that he saw much more.

- **1 Nephi 15:**
  - **Before You Read:** For the past four chapters, Nephi has been writing about the vision that followed his request to the Lord to understand his father's vision. Nephi returns from his vision in this chapter, having just witnessed the destruction of his people and eventually the end of the world.
  - **What You'll Read About:** When Nephi finishes his vision, he finds his brothers arguing over the things Lehi had taught them. Nephi teaches them that they must soften their hearts and ask the Lord to gain answers. He explains that the olive tree symbolism Lehi used referred to the house of Israel and the future of their descendants. Nephi's brothers begin to ask questions, and he teaches them the meaning of some of the symbols in Lehi's dream. He explains that there must be justice in the eternities that separates the righteous from the wicked.

# SPIRITUAL GUIDING QUESTIONS

Question: What do you notice about the role of questions in how the Spirit of the Lord teaches Nephi? (1 Nephi 11:1-23)

Question: What can we learn from Nephi's response to the angel in 1 Nephi 11:17? How can you respond when you don't yet understand parts of God's plan? (1 Nephi 11:16-17)

Question: How has the word of God led you to better understand and feel the love of God? (1 Nephi 11:25)

Question: What do you notice about the size of the areas where the wicked are found in Lehi's vision? What does that teach us about God's path vs. the world's paths? (1 Nephi 12:16-18)

Question: What blessing did Nephi learn would be available to us in our time? How can you do a little better at qualifying for that blessing? (1 Nephi 13:37)

Question: What is the purpose of God preserving the Book of Mormon? How has your own testimony of the Book of Mormon grown and changed over time? (1 Nephi 13:40-41)

Question: When is a time in your life that you have inquired of the Lord and received an answer? What was that experience like? (1 Nephi 15:8)

# 1 NEPHI 16 - 22

## *"I Will Prepare the Way before You"*

# BIG PICTURE

*How to feel confident fitting in this week's readings with the entire Book of Mormon*

## General Context:

- **Just like that, we finishing the First Book of Nephi.** Nephi is writing this record many years in the future. In fact, in chapter 19 this week, we'll read that Nephi wrote so much more detail and history on the other plates that we don't have. While I would love to know all the extra details and events that he had to leave out in this smaller record, it also makes the few details and stories carry much more weight- Nephi clearly took his call seriously to write a record that would be a sacred record and point people to Christ. There are lots of important stories and events that happen in these chapters, including:
  - Lehi finds a special compass that only works through their faith
  - Nephi breaks his bow while hunting
  - Nephi is commanded to build a ship
  - The group crosses the sea in the ship
  - They all arrive in the promised land
  - Nephi quotes lots of scripture and teaches about God's covenant people
- **What's the timeline here?** It's easy to gloss over the fact that Lehi's group stayed in the wilderness for 8 years prior to arriving in Bountiful on the coast, where they likely stayed even longer before getting on the boat. Since Lehi initially left Jerusalem in 600 B.C., they arrived in Bountiful on the coast in 592 B.C. The next time marker Nephi tells us doesn't come until 2 Nephi chapter 5, where he says the 30 years had passed since first leaving Jerusalem (570 B.C.). So the events of building the ship, crossing the sea, and initially arriving in the promised land happened any time between 8 and 30 years after first leaving Jerusalem.

- **Do I spy some Isaiah?** You've got this. Two chapters (1 Nephi 20 and 1 Nephi 21) this week include Nephi quoting from Isaiah chapters 48-49. But Nephi gives us so much help in chapter 22 as he explains and puts into his own words what he just read from Isaiah.
- Basically, both Nephi and Isaiah are talking about God's covenant relationship with His people. We know that the covenant began with Abraham, blossoming into the covenant "children of Israel". The children of the covenant were not keeping their faith with sincere hearts, and so God needed to scatter them both physically and spiritually, with the sure promise that they would be gathered again and learn about Jesus Christ.
- As a side note, when most people refer to "the Isaiah chapters", they are actually referring to 2 Nephi chapters 12-24. This is just a quick little dip in the water for Isaiah in the Book of Mormon.

# Spiritual Themes:

Look for these themes as you read the chapters this week! Find examples in the scriptures, and ponder on what these themes can look like in your life.

- **Working with God to solve problems**

- **Humble obedience vs. prideful rebellion**

- **God's relationship with His covenant people**

# People to Know:

- **Nephi**
  - He married one of the daughters of Ishmael. He breaks his bow and prayerfully makes an effort to repair the situation. Once in Bountiful, Nephi is commanded to build a ship. He first makes the tools and then builds the boat with the help of his family. While crossing the ocean, Laman and Lemuel tie Nephi up. We learn that Nephi's wife and children pleaded for his life. They eventually make it to the promised land. Nephi quotes and explains scripture to his family.
- **Laman**
  - Nephi's older brother, he married one of the daughters of Ishmael. He got angry at Nephi for breaking his bow, for trying to build a ship, and then while crossing the sea.
- **Lemuel**
  - Nephi's older brother, he married one of the daughters of Ishmael. He got angry at Nephi for breaking his bow, for trying to build a ship, and then while crossing the sea.
- **Sam**
  - He married one of the daughters of Ishmael. Sam was righteous and generally followed Lehi and Nephi's lead.

- **Zoram**
  - Zoram was Laban's servant who ended up going with Nephi's family after helping them obtain the records of the Jews. He married one of the daughters of Ishmael.
- **Lehi**
  - Lehi heard the Lord command him that they should leave the valley of Lemuel and start on their journey. He finds a compass in front of his tent. After Nephi breaks his bow, even Lehi becomes angry. Lehi repents and is humbled by the writing on the compass, and by Nephi's preaching. Lehi and Sariah are getting old by the time they cross the ocean to the promised land.
- **Ishmael**
  - Ishmael was a resident in Jerusalem who ended up going with Lehi's family into the wilderness. Ishmael's family included his wife, their 5 daughters, and their 2 sons. Some of his daughters married the children of Lehi, including Nephi. Ishmael died and was buried in Nahom.
- **Jacob**
  - Jacob was Nephi's younger brother who was born at some point during their many years in the wilderness.
- **Joseph**
  - Joseph was Nephi's younger brother, even younger than Jacob, who was born at some point during their many years in the wilderness.

# Where are We?

- **Wilderness**
  - Lehi's family, Ishmael's family, and Zoram have been in the wilderness in the Valley of Lemuel. They stay here until Lehi hears the voice of the Lord command him to keep traveling in the wilderness. They journey in the wilderness, making some stops, for the next eight years before reaching Bountiful.
- **Nahom**
  - Nahom was a place the traveling families encountered during their journey in the wilderness. Ishmael died and was buried here.
- **Bountiful**
  - Bountiful was a land on the sea filled with fruits and wild honey. The group came and lived here after journeying in the wilderness for eight years. This is where Nephi is commanded to build a ship, and where the group lives while preparing for their journey to the Promised Land.
- **Promised Land**
  - After sailing in the boat that Nephi and his brothers built, the group arrives in the promised land. They notice that the promised land has lots of animals and natural resources.

# LITTLE PICTURE

*How to understand each chapter and apply principles to my life*

- **1 Nephi 16:**
  - **Before You Read:** In the previous chapter, Nephi had just finished receiving his vision and was then teaching his brothers about the meaning behind some of the symbols in Lehi's vision. Nephi finished by talking about the fate that awaits the unrepentant wicked.
  - **What You'll Read About:** Nephi tells his brothers that the wicked take the truth to be hard, and his brothers humble themselves. Nephi, his brothers, and Zoram (Laban's servant) marry the daughters of Ishmael. Lehi receives revelation that they should leave into the wilderness, finds a compass outside of his tent, and they depart. While hunting, Nephi breaks his bow, meaning the group can't get the food they need. Everyone complains, but Nephi prays and is able to make a new bow. They discover the compass works according to their faith, and Nephi hunts beasts. Ishmael dies and is buried. The daughters of Ishmael complain, and Laman and Lemuel plan to kill Lehi and Nephi so they can return to Jerusalem. The Lord chastens them and they repent.

- **1 Nephi 17:**
  - **Before You Read:** In the previous chapter, Ishmael died, causing his daughters, Laman, and Lemuel to complain and plot against Lehi. They were chastened by the Lord and repented.
  - **What You'll Read About:** The group prospers in the wilderness and lives there for eight years. They come to a beautiful place by the sea called Bountiful, where the Lord commands Nephi to build a ship so the group can sail to a new promised land. Nephi's brothers complain against Nephi and Lehi while Nephi makes the tools to build a ship. Nephi reminds them of the way God has delivered and blessed the children of Israel because of their righteousness. He shows them the pattern of God protecting those who worship Him. He chastises his brothers, and they want to throw him into the sea. He is filled with the power of God, and they are scared to touch him for days. Nephi touches them, and God shows His power by shocking them. They believe him and try to worship Nephi.

- **1 Nephi 18:**
  - **Before You Read:** In the previous chapter, Nephi was commanded to build a ship. Nephi shocked his brothers, so they repented and were willing to help.
  - **What You'll Read About:** Nephi and his brothers build the ship with the direction from the Lord. They gather provisions and begin to sail in their ship to the promised land. On the ship, Nephi rebukes his brothers for their rude behavior, causing Laman and Lemuel to tie him up with cords. The compass stops working and they are driven back by a tempest for four days before they decide to loosen Nephi's bands and repent out of fear. They sail for many days and finally arrive in the promised land. They begin to plant seeds and notice all the abundance of resources in the land.

- **1 Nephi 19:**
  - **Before You Read:** Lehi's family just arrived in the promised land after a long journey in their ship. In this chapter, Nephi references some books of scripture from prophets in Jerusalem that we no longer have a record of, including Zenock, Neum, and Zenos.
  - **What You'll Read About:** Nephi makes plates of ore to engrave a record of his people and his father's record (he has not yet made the plates we are reading from). Nephi testifies of Jesus Christ and prophesies of His sacrifice and death. He reads from the plates of brass and teaches his brothers many things about the history of God's people. He likens the scriptures to their lives.

- **1 Nephi 20:**
  - **Before You Read:** In the previous chapter, Nephi studied the brass plates and taught them to his family. He taught that the words of Isaiah teach of Jesus Christ. In this chapter, he quotes the scriptures that we know as Isaiah 48.
  - **What You'll Read About:** The Lord is refining Israel in the furnace of affliction. He has always revealed His plans to the prophets, but most people have not listened. The Lord comforts Israel when they keep the commandments. The Lord commands Israel to leave Babylon.

- **1 Nephi 21:**
    - **Before You Read:** Nephi just quoted Isaiah 48, which taught that the Lord will always reveal His plans to the prophets. In this chapter, Nephi quotes the scripture that we know as Isaiah 49.
    - **What You'll Read About:** Isaiah laments that he hasn't been able to change many hearts with his message and that it has all been in vain. The Savior promises that He will never forget us and will continue to work with us. Israel will all be gathered together.

- **1 Nephi 22:**
    - **Before You Read:** Nephi just read from Isaiah 48 and 49, teaching his family about how God will never forget His covenant people. Nephi will now explain and expound on what Isaiah just taught.
    - **What You'll Read About:** Nephi teaches that the house of Israel will be scattered among all nations and led away both spiritually and temporally. The house of Israel will then be gathered together again, and all who fight against it will be destroyed. Nephi prophesies about a time when the righteous will be preserved and the wicked destroyed. Satan will have no power and Christ will reign. Nephi testifies that the things written on the brass plates are true.

# SPIRITUAL GUIDING QUESTIONS

Question: How does studying about the "curious ball" leading Lehi's family teach you about how God can give direction in your life today? (1 Nephi 16:16)

Question: What did Nephi do after he made a very costly mistake? How did his actions and attitude help strengthen the faith of the people around him and help solve the problem at the same time? (1 Nephi 16:23)

Question: Compare 1 Nephi 17:2 with 1 Nephi 17:20. These describe the same situation from two different perspectives. What does that tell you about the way your perspective can change your experience? (1 Nephi 17:2, 20)

Question: If a mountain symbolizes our current temples, what can you learn about what God wanted Nephi to do prior to giving him new revelation? (1 Nephi 17:7-8)

Question: What obvious miracles had many in Lehi's group been living with for years at this point? What is a consistent miracle in your life that you might be overlooking? (1 Nephi 17:12-13)

Question: Knowing what Nephi's brothers will do in the future, how does what they say to Nephi differ from true conversion? How can you make sure you are truly converted? (1 Nephi 17:55)

Question: Why would you want your peace compared to a river? What qualities of a river would be desirable in the peace we feel? (1 Nephi 20:18)

# 2 NEPHI 1 - 2

### *"Free to Choose Liberty and Eternal Life, through the Great Mediator"*

# BIG PICTURE

*How to feel confident fitting in this week's readings with the entire New Testament*

## General Context:

- **Are you ready to dive into some beautiful and hopeful doctrine and advice?!** If I had to give an overall theme to the entire Second Book of Nephi, I would say that it is focused on teachings about Jesus Christ. 1 Nephi was filled with a lot of action with Nephi telling all of the often dramatic stories that brought their group to the promised land. And now, Nephi will present the most important spiritual teachings that he wants to preserve in 2 Nephi. To be clear, there are still some stories that we get in 2 Nephi. But the emphasis is on the doctrine being taught.

- **The Second Book of Nephi picks up right where we left off in 1 Nephi.** Lehi and Sariah's family, Ishmael's family (although Ishmael had died), and Zoram (now married to Ishmael's daughter) have now arrived in the promised land. Nephi had just taught his family from the words of Isaiah and shared his own testimony about God keeping His covenant relationship with His people.

- **And I assume Nephi is still the author of 2 Nephi?** The simple answer is yes, but there are some caveats. **While Nephi is the author, he quotes extensively from other people, such as Lehi, his brother Jacob, and Isaiah, throughout this record.** So pay attention as you begin each chapter to who is actually speaking! And don't worry, I'll always help you out here in each week's study guide, and you can check out each chapter in the "Little Picture" portion for more details.

- **So is Nephi quoting anyone this week?** Actually, the two chapters that we study this week are almost exclusively quoting Lehi. Lehi is going to share counsel with his family members. These teachings will continue into next week's assignment, too, so keep an eye out for more advice from Lehi in the future. We know that Lehi is toward the end of his life at this point. Lehi had struggled physically during the crossing of the ocean, and it has been around 30 years since their family first left Jerusalem. As you read Lehi's teachings to his family members, consider the wisdom, life experience, and perspective that he wanted to share before he knew his mortal life would end. Lehi gives counsel to:
  - Laman, Lemuel, Sam, the sons of Ishamel, and Zoram in 2 Nephi 1
  - Jacob in 2 Nephi 2
  - Joseph in 2 Nephi 3 (we'll study this next week)

# Spiritual Themes:

Look for these themes as you read the chapters this week! Find examples in the scriptures, and ponder on what these themes can look like in your life.

- **Current choices affecting generations in the future**

- **Opposition in all things**

- **The freedom to choose**

# People to Know:

- **Nephi:**
  - Nephi, the author of this book, had arrived in the promised land with his family. He is writing these small plates specifically with the things that will strengthen his reader's belief in Jesus Christ. In these chapters, he will share what his father taught in his final teachings and blessings to his family.
- **Lehi:**
  - Lehi is toward the end of his life at this point. He gathers his extended family together to teach them the final lessons and principles that he wants them to know. He pleads with Laman and Lemuel to listen to Nephi. He praises Zoram for being a good friend to Nephi. And he gives specific counsel to his son Jacob.
- **Laman:**
  - Laman is Nephi's oldest brother. His father counsels him to humble himself and listen to Nephi, who isn't trying to just gain power over him.

- **Lemuel:**
  - Lemuel is Nephi's older brother. His father counsels him to listen to Nephi.
- **Sam:**
  - Sam is Nephi's older brother. While he generally follows his father's counsel, Lehi tells him to make sure he listens to Nephi.
- **Jacob:**
  - Jacob is Nephi's younger brother who was born during the period of time that the group journeyed in the wilderness. Lehi specifically addresses Jacob in chapter 2.
- **Ishmael's sons and daughters:**
  - While Ishmael died prior to them traveling to the promised land, many of his children had married Lehi's children. Lehi counsels them to listen to Nephi, too.
- **Zoram:**
  - Zoram was Laban's servant who ended up going with Nephi's family after helping them obtain the records of the Jews. He married one of the daughters of Ishmael. We learn in these chapters that Zoram has become a good friend to Nephi, and Lehi promises his posterity great prosperity.

# Where are We?

- **The Land of First Inheritance**
  - Now in the promised land, Lehi's family originally puts down their roots in an area that they refer to as the "land of their first inheritance." Looking to the future, this will eventually become a home for the Lamanites after the righteous people leave.

# LITTLE PICTURE

*How to understand each chapter and apply principles to my life*

- **2 Nephi 1:**
  - **Before You Read:** Even though this is a new book, 2 Nephi picks up exactly where 1 Nephi ends! Nephi had just finished teaching and prophesying to his brothers. In this chapter, look for Nephi quoting extensively from his father Lehi's teachings to his family.
  - **What You'll Read About:** Lehi teaches that Jerusalem has been destroyed, and prophesies that the promised land will be a land of liberty for people of God. He teaches that the righteous will prosper in the land, while the wicked will perish. Lehi pleads with his posterity to be unified and live in righteousness. He asks Laman, Lemuel, and the others to listen to their brother Nephi because they will not be led astray with him.

- **2 Nephi 2:**
  - **Before You Read:** Lehi is giving his final address and advice to all those who have traveled to the promised land together. In the previous chapter, he counseled them to be righteous and listen to Nephi.
  - **What You'll Read About:** Lehi addresses his son Jacob and teaches that salvation and redemption come through our Savior. He teaches that there must be opposition in all things. An angel fell from heaven and became the devil who tempted Adam and Eve. This life is a time of probation to repent and prepare. Lehi teaches about the importance of the Fall of Adam and Eve in God's plan. We are free to choose liberty and eternal life through our Savior.

# SPIRITUAL GUIDING QUESTIONS

Question: Why do you think Lehi reminded Nephi's brothers of their rebellions and the Lord's mercy? Why is it important to remember our own mistakes in order to see God's hand in our lives? (2 Nephi 1:2-5)

Question: Lehi implores his family to awaken from a deep sleep. What do you think it might look like to be spiritually asleep? How do we wake up from that sleep? (2 Nephi 1:13-15, 23)

Question: What is the difference between the way Laman and Lemuel perceived Nephi and his real intentions? What could you learn from this misunderstanding? (2 Nephi 1:25-26)

Question: What do you think it means when Lehi teaches that "salvation is free"? (2 Nephi 2:4)

Question: Why do we need opposition in all things? When have you experienced opposing emotions or events in your life? (2 Nephi 2:11-13)

Question: What insight do you learn about Adam and Eve? How do you feel about them and their decision? (2 Nephi 2:19-25)

Question: How does agency play a role in your faith? When have you needed to actively choose to believe in Jesus Christ? (2 Nephi 2:27)

# 2 NEPHI 3 - 5

## *"We Lived After the Manner of Happiness"*

# BIG PICTURE

*How to feel confident fitting in this week's readings with the entire New Testament*

## General Context:

- **Some MAJOR EVENTS happen in these three chapters that will dramatically affect and set up the entire remainder of the Book of Mormon!** I know, I said that 2 Nephi has a lot of teaching and quoting and expounding, and while we do get a little of that in these chapters, there is also some major action:
  - **First, Lehi dies.** Lehi is truly the prophet who set this all in motion- from preaching in Jerusalem, to leading his family away to safety, to receiving much of the communication from the Lord about where to go. Not only is this a sad personal event for pretty much everyone in the promised land, but it also seems to trigger the next big event.
  - **There is the great divide into "Nephites" and "Lamanites".** Without Lehi around to smooth things over between his children anymore, the contention is ready to boil over. When Laman and Lemuel try to kill Nephi, the Lord tells Nephi that it is time to move away. Instead of living all together in one community, Nephi took everyone who wanted to stay with him (which translates to the people who had faith in the Lord) and left.
    - The people who left with Nephi to start again in a new area took the name of **Nephites.** This includes Nephi and his family, Sam and his family, Zoram and his family, and Nephi's younger brothers and sisters, including Jacob and Joseph. The focus of their civilization is to live the Law of Moses and follow God's will.
    - The people who remained in that land of first inheritance took the name of **Lamanites.** This includes Laman and his family, Lemuel and his family, and possibly any other children of Ishmael. One main focus of their civilization is that they believe Nephi wanted to gain power over them, even though he was their little brother, and that they should never have been brought to this new land. These two different viewpoints quite literally set the scene for virtually everything else that will happen in the Book of Mormon.

- **Is Nephi narrating all of this?** First, we get to hear more from Lehi. Nephi quotes Lehi in chapter 3 and about half of chapter 4. We then get Nephi telling us from his point of view what happened following his father's death. There's one more thing we can't skip over though:

- **"Nephi's lament" or "the psalm of Nephi" is in chapter 4.** Nephi writes this beautiful lament in verses 17-35 following the death of his father. You'll immediately notice the difference in tone and wording as you read these phrases from Nephi's soul. Interestingly, Nephi's words are very similar to many of the psalms we have in the Book of Psalms, specifically Psalms 25-31. These psalms are all individuals lamenting, and then praising God and referring to covenants or the temple.

- **We finally get some "time markers" in these chapters once Nephi's people had separated themselves and established their homes.** Nephi tells us that 30 years had passed since first leaving Jerusalem (and remember that we know they spent at least 8 years of that journeying in the wilderness). And then right at the end of the chapter, Nephi mentions that now 40 years have passed. This would take us to 560 B.C. by the end of chapter 5.

# Spiritual Themes:

Look for these themes as you read the chapters this week! Find examples in the scriptures, and ponder on what these themes can look like in your life.

- **Relying on the Lord for strength**

- **The Lord's abundant mercy**

- **The fruits of industrious hard work**

# People to Know:

- **Nephi**
  - Following his father's death, Nephi writes a beautiful lament expressing the feelings of his soul. When his older brothers start to plot against his life, Nephi receives revelation that he needs to leave. He travels with the people who want to stay with him and they establish a land of Nephi. Nephi leads the people in building, planting, and making things. They build a temple. Nephi is the prophet-leader.
- **Lehi**
  - Lehi gives his final counsel to his youngest son Joseph in these chapters. He gives last blessings to his grandchildren, and then Lehi dies.

- **Laman**
  - Laman is Nephi's older brother. Following Lehi's death, he plots to kill Nephi, causing Nephi and those who follow him to leave.
- **Lemuel**
  - Lemuel is Nephi's older brother who stays with Laman in the land of first inheritance when Nephi leaves.
- **Sam**
  - Sam is Nephi's older brother who follows Nephi and becomes a Nephite.
- **Jacob**
  - Jacob is Nephi's righteous younger brother who follows Nephi and becomes a Nephite. Nephi consecrates Jacob to be a priest and teacher.
- **Joseph**
  - Joseph is Nephi's righteous younger brother. Lehi addresses chapter 3 to him, and shows the significant ties of his name to other Josephs. He goes with Nephi to become a Nephite, and Nephi consecrates Joseph to be a priest and a teacher.
- **Zoram**
  - Zoram was previously Laban's servant, but now a righteous friend to Nephi. He becomes a Nephite.
- **Nephi's sisters**
  - We only get brief mention of Nephi's younger sisters, but we know that they all left for the land of Nephi and became Nephites.

# Where are We?

- *I want to add my own commentary that being very familiar with the origin of these two locations this week will help SO MUCH in adding context as we move forward in the Book of Mormon. Remember these two places!*
- **The Land of First Inheritance**
  - This is where Lehi's group initially started to build their new home. It is where the first part of 2 Nephi occurred. Lehi was buried here. However, after the righteous people leave, only the newly termed "Lamanites" remain.
- **The Land of Nephi**
  - Nephi, Zoram, Sam, Jacob, Joseph, Nephi's sisters, and all their families left their more wicked family members and traveled to this new area. They built a temple in this land.

# LITTLE PICTURE

*How to understand each chapter and apply principles to my life*

- **2 Nephi 3:**
  - **Before You Read:** Lehi had been giving his final teachings and counsel to his posterity after they reached the promised land. In the previous chapter, he taught all about opposition and Adam and Eve in his final counsel to his son Jacob. In this chapter, he will now address Joseph.
  - **What You'll Read About:** Lehi counsels Joseph, his youngest son. He teaches about their father Joseph of Egypt, teaching that Joseph saw the Nephites in a vision. He also quotes Joseph in a prophecy about another Joseph bringing forth the Book of Mormon in the last days. The Book of Mormon and the Bible will confound false doctrines. He references more of Joseph of Egypt's prophecies about Joseph of the restoration and the gathering of the house of Israel. Lehi tells young Joseph to listen to his brother Nephi.

- **2 Nephi 4:**
  - **Before You Read:** Lehi has been teaching his posterity his final lessons and giving counsel before his coming death. He just finished addressing Joseph. The end of this chapter contains what is often referred to as "Nephi's lament" or "the psalm of Nephi".
  - **What You'll Read About:** Lehi gathers the children of Laman, then Lemuel, then Ishmael, and then Sam and gives them advice and a blessing. He teaches that if they keep the commandments, they will prosper, no matter the choices of their parents. Lehi dies and is buried. Laman and Lemuel are angry with Nephi. Nephi glories in the Lord and records a beautiful psalm about his sorrow, and the consuming love of the Lord. He thanks God for redeeming him from sin and puts his trust in the Lord.

- **2 Nephi 5:**
  - **Before You Read:** Lehi just died, and we heard Nephi's beautiful psalm at the end of chapter 4.
  - **What You'll Read About:** Laman and Lemuel try to kill Nephi, so the Lord warns Nephi to flee into the wilderness. Nephi, Sam, Zoram, and Nephi's younger brothers and sisters come with him and settle in a land they call Nephi. Nephi also takes the brass plates, the compass/ball, and Laban's sword. The people of Nephi work hard to set up their land and live righteously. They build a temple and choose Nephi to be their leader. The Lord marks the people of Laman and commands them not to mix their posterity. This is finally when we hear that Nephi makes the plates that we're reading right now that contain things of spiritual importance, not just the history.

# SPIRITUAL GUIDING QUESTIONS

Question: What is the importance of a name? Does your name have any special meaning?
(2 Nephi 3)

Question: What do you notice about the final things Lehi said to each of his children?
What do you learn about God's mercy? (2 Nephi 4:3-11)

Question: What does your soul take "delight" in right now? How do you feel about the scriptures?
(2 Nephi 4:15-16)

Question: As Nephi wrestles with both overwhelming guilt and praise, how do you think we can balance recognizing our own sins while also worshiping God? (2 Nephi 4:16–20)

Question: What stands out most from Nephi's psalm as you read it? What are the phrases or words that touch your soul right now? (2 Nephi 4:16–35)

Question: What were the people of Nephi's first priorities when they moved to a new land? What can you learn from this? (2 Nephi 5:8–17)

Question: What evidence do you see for how the people of Nephi "lived after the manner of happiness"? (2 Nephi 5:27)

# 2 NEPHI 6 - 10

## "O How Great the Plan of Our God"

# BIG PICTURE

*How to feel confident fitting in this week's readings with the entire New Testament*

## General Context:

- **Are you ready to hear from Jacob?** You may have just double checked to see if we were still in 2 Nephi this week, and we are. But in chapters 6-10, we are going to read Nephi quoting the teachings of Jacob.

- **What do we know about Jacob?** Up to this point, we know that Jacob was Nephi's younger brother who was born to Lehi and Sariah while they were journeying in the wilderness outside of Jerusalem. Jacob received powerful counsel from his father in 2 Nephi 2, which contains some of the most important teachings about agency and the fall. Last week, we learned that Jacob had been consecrated by Nephi to be a priest and teacher amongst the newly separated Nephites in the land of Nephi. At least 10 years had passed since the Nephites separated themselves, so even though we don't get much narration of what occurred during that time, imagine 10 years worth of growth, building, worship, farming, and much more.

- **Ready to take it one level deeper though?** While Nephi is quoting his brother Jacob during these chapters, **Jacob also quotes extensively from Isaiah**. He is quoting portions of Isaiah 49-52, which cover prophecies that Isaiah shared about the gathering of scattered Israel. It's fascinating to think about why this small group of people, separated from their homeland and now living in a strange area, would be so interested in learning about the promised gathering of Israel. Here's what you can expect from each chapter:
  - **2 Nephi 6** – part Jacob preaching and part quoting Isaiah
  - **2 Nephi 7-8** – quoting Isaiah
  - **2 Nephi 9-19** – Jacob preaching

# Spiritual Themes:

Look for these themes as you read the chapters this week! Find examples in the scriptures, and ponder on what these themes can look like in your life.

- **Jesus Christ's atoning sacrifice**

- **The gathering of scattered Israel**

- **Rejoicing in covenant relationship with God**

# People to Know:

- **Jacob**
  - Jacob was Nephi's younger brother who was born during their journeying in the wilderness. Now that he was in the land of Nephi, Jacob was ordained and consecrated to preach to the people of Nephi as a teacher and priest. His teachings are recorded in these chapters, and we will hear more from him in the book of Jacob.
- **Isaiah**
  - Isaiah was a prophet in Jerusalem and a chief advisor to king Hezekiah. He lived about 100 years prior to Lehi and his family, when the Israelites had split into two kingdoms but had not yet been conquered. He prophesied about the scattering of Israel, the coming of the Messiah, and the eventual gathering of Israel.

# Where are We?

- **The Land of Nephi**
  - Nephi and the other righteous members of his family had separated themselves and established their new home in a place they called the land of Nephi. It was first established right before 570 B.C. The people were industrious and built up the land, including constructing a temple.

# LITTLE PICTURE

*How to understand each chapter and apply principles to my life*

- **2 Nephi 6:**
  - **Before You Read:** In the last few chapters, we learned that Lehi died, there was a big split in the family, and Nephi had separated himself from Laman and Lemuel (along with the other family members who believed him). The new land of Nephi had been established, and Nephi had consecrated Jacob and Joseph as priests and teachers. In this chapter, Nephi quotes Jacob teaching. Jacob also quotes Isaiah twice in this chapter.
  - **What You'll Read About:** Nephi's brother Jacob teaches the people of Nephi that he wants to teach them Isaiah's words, because they are about the house of Israel. Jacob quotes from Isaiah 49 and prophesies that Jerusalem has already been destroyed and the people carried away. But he knows that the Israelites will be allowed to return again. Jacob expounds with his own prophecies of Jesus Christ being born and crucified in Jerusalem. He teaches that those who fight against Zion will suffer, while those who repent and believe in Christ will be delivered.

- **2 Nephi 7:**
  - **Before You Read:** In the previous chapter, Jacob taught the people of Nephi from the words of Isaiah about the scattering and gathering of Israel. Jacob quotes Isaiah 50 in this chapter.
  - **What You'll Read About:** Jacob quotes Isaiah teaching about how the Lord has not gone anywhere- it is the people who are choosing to reject Him. Isaiah has not been rebellious, which means he will be shown mercy. The Lord should be the light, instead of people trying to make their own light.

- **2 Nephi 8:**
  - **Before You Read:** Jacob has been teaching the people of Nephi from the words of Isaiah. He continues by quoting from Isaiah 51 and the first two verses of 52 in this chapter.
  - **What You'll Read About:** The Lord reminds His people of their spiritual heritage that they can draw strength from. He will always comfort those who need help and call upon Him, which means His people have no need to fear their enemies. There will be so much joy when Israel is gathered together and people turn back to the Lord.

- **2 Nephi 9:**

  - **Before You Read:** Jacob just finished quoting from Isaiah, sharing teachings about the gathering of Israel. In this chapter, Jacob will now speak. Look for both Jacob's powerful testimony and the important doctrines he emphasizes.

  - **What You'll Read About:** Jacob teaches that the house of Israel will be gathered, and that Christ will perform an infinite atonement to save mankind. He teaches about spiritual death, and the merciful plan of God to deliver us. In the next life, the righteous will stay righteous and the wicked will stay wicked. God commands us to repent and be baptized. Those without the law will be saved as well. Jacob condemns the learned, the rich, and anyone who allows things to separate themselves from God. Come unto God with humility and He will open the gate. Pray unto God daily with gratitude.

- **2 Nephi 10:**

  - **Before You Read:** Jacob has been teaching about God's great plan of salvation which is made possible through the sacrifice of Jesus Christ. This is the end of Jacob's sermon.

  - **What You'll Read About:** Jacob teaches that Christ will live among the Jews in Jerusalem and be crucified. He prophesies about the scattering and gathering of Israel, and that their land (the Americas) would become a land of liberty for the Gentiles. He teaches that even though they have been led away from the rest of the house of Israel, God still remembers them. He instructs them to cheer up their hearts because they are free to act for themselves.

# SPIRITUAL GUIDING QUESTIONS

Question: What does Jacob teach the people first? Why do you think he does that?
(2 Nephi 6:1-5)

Question: How have you separated yourself from God at times in your life? What has it looked like to grow closer to God again? (2 Nephi 7:1-2)

Question: What does it mean to you that God will make Zion's wilderness like Eden? What has that looked like in your life? (2 Nephi 8:3)

Question: What do you learn about covenants from Jacob and Isaiah's teachings? (2 Nephi 9:1)

Question: Why was an infinite atonement necessary? (2 Nephi 9:7)

Question: What does this chapter teach us about what will happen to us after we die? How can this give you a new perspective on a current struggle? (2 Nephi 9:13-18)

Question: How does the doctrine in these verses cheer up your heart? (2 Nephi 10:23-25)

# 2 NEPHI 11 - 19

## "His Name Shall Be Called... The Prince of Peace"

# BIG PICTURE

*How to feel confident fitting in this week's readings with the entire Book of Mormon*

## General Context:

- **Nephi is now going to share some teachings that he wants to send out to all of the Nephites.** You'll remember that Nephi just finished quoting his brother Jacob's sermon, and now Nephi is recording his own thoughts that he really wants all of his people to hear. **This section also begins what is commonly referred to as "the Isaiah chapters"** (we will finish them up next week).

- **Let's ask the question we have all wondered about: Why did Nephi quote so much from Isaiah?!** It's easy to think of Isaiah as some old prophet who wrote down a bunch of confusing prophecies– but let's take a look at who the man Isaiah really was. Allow me to share some context that I think might help you realize why Nephi sharing Isaiah actually makes perfect sense:

  ○ **Isaiah lived in Jerusalem when the Israelites had been split into the northern kingdom and the southern kingdom.** Isaiah served from 740-701 B.C. with many kings, but was the chief advisor to king Hezekiah, who reigned in Jerusalem over the southern kingdom of Judah. Hezekiah was a righteous king, unlike his father, wicked king Ahaz. Isaiah seemed to become a good friend to Hezekiah, and the kingdom of Judah made huge improvements in turning toward the Lord.

  ○ **It was during this time that the northern kingdom started to fall to the Assyrians, and the scattering of Israel began.** Lehi's ancestors from the tribe of Manasseh would have presumably escaped from the Assyrians and settled in Jerusalem. The Assyrians soon started marching toward Jerusalem, but Isaiah prophesied that Jerusalem would be spared. They were, and Judah was left standing, for now.

  ○ **It is in the backdrop of this chaos that Isaiah received and recorded numerous prophecies.** Many of his prophecies were about either the inevitable scattering of Israel, the coming of Jesus Christ to Jerusalem, the eventual restoration and gathering of Israel, or Jesus' Second Coming during the last days.

- Isaiah lived and prophesied about 100 years before the story of the Book of Mormon begins with Lehi's family. Think of a prophet who served about 100 years ago from right now- Isaiah wasn't a "super old prophet" to them! He was extremely relevant.
- Lehi's family needed Isaiah's teachings to comfort them. Just think- Lehi's family had been asked to leave Jerusalem, journey in the wilderness, and sail across to the sea to a land they didn't even know existed. As they start to build a whole new society, imagine the feelings of loneliness and insecurity that they may have felt. And yet, Isaiah's words reminded them that they were not alone. God had a purpose in scattering Israel, and in fact, Jerusalem had already fallen and been scattered at this point. Isaiah's writings are filled with hope for their future, and pointed the Nephites toward their Savior, who they knew would live in Jerusalem, but would visit them. All this to say- Isaiah's words were extremely relevant and uplifting for these Nephites.
- And as we study Isaiah's teachings more and more, I think we will find his words relevant and uplifting for our day too, in the thick of the restoration and the gathering of scattered Israel.
- Are these all Isaiah chapters this week? Pretty much. Here's how they line up:
  - Chapter 11: We read Nephi's words introducing Isaiah
  - Chapters 12-19: Nephi quotes Isaiah chapters 2-9

# Spiritual Themes:

Look for these themes as you read the chapters this week! Find examples in the scriptures, and ponder on what these themes can look like in your life.

- Repentance through Jesus Christ

- Having humility or being humbled

- Ultimate blessings for the righteous

# People to Know:

- Nephi
  - Nephi is the prophet-leader for the land of Nephi. After his brothers tried to kill him, Nephi and the people who trusted him separated themselves from Laman and Lemuel and started their own land. Nephi becomes their political and spiritual leader, consecrating priests and teachers and making sure everyone learned of Jesus. In the chapters this week, Nephi is going to preach and share the words of Isaiah that he wants his people to hear.

- **Jacob**
  - Jacob is Nephi's younger brother who had been called as a teacher and priest among the people. Nephi just finished sharing one of Jacob's sermons. We also learn in chapter 11 that Jacob saw his Redeemer, just as Nephi did.
- **Isaiah**
  - Isaiah was a prophet in Jerusalem and a chief advisor to king Hezekiah for about 40 years, from 740-701 B.C. This means that he lived about 100 years prior to Lehi and his family, when the Israelites had split into two kingdoms but had not yet been conquered. He prophesied about the scattering of Israel, the coming of the Messiah, and the eventual gathering of Israel.
- **King Uzziah**
  - Mentioned in Isaiah's teachings, Uzziah was the king of Judah, the southern kingdom, when Isaiah was first called as a prophet. He was righteous for most of his life but had a problem with pride toward the end of his reign.
- **King Ahaz**
  - Mentioned in Isaiah's teachings, Ahaz was the king of Judah, two kings after his grandfather Uzziah. He was very wicked and ended up aligning the kingdom with the Assyrians, even after seeing the Assyrians completely destroy and carry away Israel to the north, and being warned by the Lord through Isaiah not to do that.

# Where are We?

- **The Land of Nephi**
  - Nephi and the other righteous members of his family had separated themselves from Laman and Lemuel and established their new home in a place they called the land of Nephi. It was first established right before 570 B.C. The people were industrious and built up the land, including constructing a temple.

**In the quoted Isaiah chapters, here are some locations to know:**
- **Judah**
  - Also known as the southern kingdom, Judah had the capital city of Jerusalem and housed the temple where Isaiah served. This was also the home of king Uzziah and king Ahaz. Judah was threatened by attacks from northern Israel and Syria, and it was prophesied that Assyria would capture many of their lands, but not all. Over 100 years after these prophecies were written (and after Lehi and his family left), Judah fell to the Babylonians, and the people were scattered.

- **Israel**
  - Israel was the name of the northern kingdom, with Samaria as its capital. It is sometimes referred to as Ephraim. Isaiah prophesied that Israel/Ephraim/Samaria would fall to the Assyrians. Israel also attempted to team up with Syria to attack Judah.
- **Assyria**
  - The Assyrians destroyed northern Israel and started the official scattering of Israel. Judah aligned themselves with Assyria to try to save themselves, and ended up owing them a large tribute. Although Assyria was allowed to conquer Israel, they were eventually conquered as retribution from the Lord.

# LITTLE PICTURE

*How to understand each chapter and apply principles to my life*

- **2 Nephi 11:**
  - **Before You Read:** Nephi had been quoting his brother Jacob's teachings for the past few chapters. In this chapter, Nephi concludes Jacob's teachings and gives a little introduction to what he will write next.
  - **What You'll Read About:** Nephi writes that he will quote more of the words of Isaiah because Isaiah testifies of Christ. Nephi and Jacob have both seen the Savior. Nephi shares that teaching his people about Jesus brings him joy. The Law of Moses points them to Christ. He invites his people to liken the words of Isaiah to themselves.

- **2 Nephi 12:**
  - **Before You Read:** In this chapter, Nephi quotes from the words of Isaiah chapter 2. This chapter is a prophecy about the latter days and the Second Coming.
  - **What You'll Read About:** The temple, a place of learning, will be established, and everyone will want to attend. The people who choose to forget the Lord will be forced to be humbled when Jesus comes.

- **2 Nephi 13:**
  - **Before You Read:** Nephi quotes Isaiah 3. He talks about Judah and Jerusalem in this chapter, which both represent the house of Israel.
  - **What You'll Read About:** The wicked will be punished for their disobedience, but the righteous will be blessed at the same time. The Lord will go to judge the people, and they will still be prideful and oppressive.

- **2 Nephi 14:**
  - **Before You Read:** In the previous chapter, Nephi quoted as Isaiah taught about the wicked who forget the Lord and are caught up in pride. This chapter quotes Isaiah 4.
  - **What You'll Read About:** After the filth has been purged from Zion, the earth will be made beautiful again, and the Lord will set up a protective place for all the righteous.

- **2 Nephi 15:**
  - **Before You Read:** Nephi has been quoting Isaiah. This chapter quotes Isaiah 5.
  - **What You'll Read About:** Isaiah uses a metaphor of a vineyard to finish up his teachings about the consequences of forgetting the Lord. He prophesies that the vineyard will become desolate and get taken into captivity. The people still do not humble themselves and receive more chastening.

- **2 Nephi 16:**
  - **Before You Read:** In the last few chapters of Isaiah that Nephi has quoted, Isaiah taught about the consequences of forgetting the Lord. This chapter quotes Isaiah 6.
  - **What You'll Read About:** Isaiah tells the story of how he was called to be a prophet by the Lord. King Uzziah was the king of Judah, and Isaiah was in the temple. He felt inadequate to be called, but his sins were forgiven and he volunteered to serve the Lord.

- **2 Nephi 17:**
  - **Before You Read:** Isaiah had told the story of being called as a prophet when Uzziah was the king of Judah. In this chapter, Nephi continues to quote Isaiah 7, so here's some context for the events you'll read about: King Ahaz was the grandson of Uzziah, king of the southern kingdom of Judah. The northern kingdom of Israel is often referred to as "Ephraim" in the Old Testament, since the tribe of Ephraim had the dominant role in Israel.
  - **What You'll Read About:** Isaiah delivers the news to king Ahaz that the northern kingdom of Israel is teaming up with Syria to come against Judah. The Lord wants Ahaz to do nothing, and trust that the battle will fizzle out, but Ahaz refuses to believe that. The Lord wants Ahaz to ask for a sign, but Ahaz doesn't want that either. Isaiah prophesies of a sign anyway, teaching about the future arrival of the Savior through a virgin mother.

- **2 Nephi 18:**
  - **Before You Read:** In the previous chapter (quoting from Isaiah), Isaiah had been prophesying to king Ahaz about the destruction of both Israel and Judah by Assyria. He also started to prophesy of Christ's birth. This chapter quotes Isaiah 8.
  - **What You'll Read About:** Isaiah mentions his wife and his son. The Lord teaches that both Israel and Judah will be attacked by the Assyrians, although Judah will be spared from total destruction for now. Christ will be a safe place for those who believe, but a stumbling stone for those who do not trust in Him.

- **2 Nephi 19:**
  - **Before You Read:** Isaiah has been prophesying about the captivity and destruction of both Israel and Judah, and teaching about the Savior. This chapter quotes Isaiah 9.
  - **What You'll Read About:** After the great damage from being captured by the Assyrians, there will be relief and light. A Savior will come to rule the government with peace. Despite all of this, the people will rebel.

# SPIRITUAL GUIDING QUESTIONS

Question: Why does Nephi say he shares the words of Isaiah? How are you able to do what Nephi asked his people to do, too? (2 Nephi 11:8)

Question: Why does God need to humble us continually? When is a time you have been humbled? (2 Nephi 12:7-12)

Question: How does Isaiah respond when the Lord calls him to be a prophet? When is a time in your life you were asked to do something overwhelming? (2 Nephi 16:5-11)

Question: Changing and repenting can sometimes be painful. Why do you think it is still worth it to try to change over and over again in your life? (2 Nephi 16:6-7)

Question: How does Ahaz respond when the Lord wants him to ask for a sign? Why is it important for us to pray and ask for things from the Lord? (2 Nephi 17:10-12)

Question: How is the Lord a sanctuary, or a safe place, to you? How have you seen Him be a stumbling block for other people? (2 Nephi 18:14)

Question: What is a name of Christ that stands out to you? Why is that role important to you? (2 Nephi 19:6)

# 2 NEPHI 20 -25

## *"We Rejoice in Christ"*

# BIG PICTURE

*How to feel confident fitting in this week's readings with the entire New Testament*

## General Context:

- **It probably won't surprise you to learn that Isaiah is the most quoted prophet in scripture!** The Book of Mormon AND the Doctrine and Covenants both quote Isaiah more than any other prophet. Paul, Peter, and John in the New Testament also quote Isaiah more than anyone else. And even Jesus Christ quoted Isaiah more than any other prophet. The themes and prophecies that Isaiah writes about are important, and applicable to everyone!

- **This week, we will finish up hearing from Isaiah, and then Nephi will start to share his own commentary.** Nephi started writing his own teachings back in chapter 11. In chapters 20-24, Nephi will quote Isaiah 10-14. In chapter 25, Nephi will start to explain Isaiah's teachings and give customized counsel to those listening. Looking forward, Nephi will continue to write his own teachings, prophecies, and counsel until the end of 2 Nephi, which has 33 chapters.

- **These Isaiah chapters are mostly focused on Christ's Second Coming.** Isaiah will use "Babylon" to represent everyone who is not with the Lord, which makes sense because the real Babylonians were the ones who eventually conquered Jerusalem, completely scattering Israel. He will also use "Israel", "Samaria", "Jerusalem", or "Judah" to represent the Lord's covenant people of any dispensation. However, instead of worrying too much about every single point of context, I would encourage you to focus on how these concepts connect to BOTH the Nephites, and to us in the latter days. How are the warnings about the destruction of Babylon applicable today? Why do we care what happens to Israel and Judah?

# Spiritual Themes:

Look for these themes as you read the chapters this week! Find examples in the scriptures, and ponder on what these themes can look like in your life.

- **Praising the Lord**

- **Choosing to be God's covenant people**

- **Pointing others to Christ**

# People to Know:

- **Nephi**
  - Nephi is the prophet-leader for the land of Nephi. After his brothers tried to kill him, Nephi and the people who trusted him separated themselves and started their own land. Nephi consecrated priests and teachers and made sure everyone learned of Jesus. In the chapters this week, Nephi is going to share even more words from Isaiah, and then start to add his own commentary.

- **Isaiah**
  - Isaiah was a prophet in Jerusalem and a chief advisor to king Hezekiah for about 40 years, from 740-701 B.C. This means that he lived about 100 years prior to Lehi and his family. In these chapters, Isaiah will speak with king Ahaz about future events for both Israel and Judah, prophesying about their inevitable destruction. Isaiah is alive for when the northern kingdom of Israel is taken captive by the Assyrians, and he also witnesses the Assyrians take over much of the southern kingdom of Judah, although Jerusalem is spared at the time. He assists king Hezekiah by speaking with the Lord on his behalf. According to tradition, Isaiah is killed by an ax during wicked king Manasseh's reign, although there is no scriptural record of his death.

- **King Ahaz**
  - Mentioned in Isaiah's teachings, Ahaz was a king of Judah. He was very wicked and ended up aligning the kingdom with the Assyrians, even after seeing the Assyrians completely destroy and carry away Israel to the north, and being warned by the Lord through Isaiah not to do that.

# Where are We?

- **The Land of Nephi**
  - Nephi and the other righteous members of his family had separated themselves and established their new home in a place they called the land of Nephi. It was first established right before 570 B.C. The people were industrious and built up the land, including constructing a temple. This is where Nephi is as he records his teachings.

**In the quoted Isaiah chapters, here are some locations to know:**
- **Judah**
  - Also known as the southern kingdom, Judah had the capital city of Jerusalem and housed the temple where Isaiah served. This was also the home of king Uzziah and king Ahaz. Judah was threatened by attacks from northern Israel and Syria, and it was prophesied that Assyria would capture many of their lands, but not all. Over 100 years after these prophecies were written (and after Lehi and his family left), Judah fell to the Babylonians and the people were scattered.
- **Israel**
  - Israel was the name of the northern kingdom, with Samaria as its capital. It is sometimes referred to as Ephraim. Isaiah prophesied that Israel/Ephraim/Samaria would fall to the Assyrians. Israel also attempted to team up with Syria to attack Judah.
- **Assyria**
  - The Assyrians destroyed northern Israel and started the official scattering of Israel. Judah aligned themselves with Assyria to try to save themselves and ended up owing them a large tribute. Although Assyria was allowed to conquer Israel, they were eventually conquered as retribution from the Lord.
- **Babylon**
  - Babylon was a large nation in the Mesopotamia area, east of Israel. It is the same location as Babel (think: Tower of Babel). Babylon eventually captured Judah and carried them away captive. Babylon is often used as a metaphor for anything worldly, or people who put their trust in man over God.

# LITTLE PICTURE

*How to understand each chapter and apply principles to my life*

- **2 Nephi 20:**
  - **Before You Read:** Nephi has been quoting the words of Isaiah and will continue to do so in this chapter. Isaiah has been prophesying about Israel and Judah and their threats from Assyria. This chapter quotes Isaiah 10
  - **What You'll Read About:** The leaders of Israel are forgetting the poor and the needy, so the Assyrians will be able to take over their lands. But then the Assyrians will be destroyed for their unrighteousness, too. A small remnant of righteous people will be able to thrive because they turn to the Lord.

- **2 Nephi 21:**
  - **Before You Read:** Isaiah just finished prophesying about how Assyria would also be destroyed after being allowed to conquer Israel and Judah. This chapter quotes Isaiah 11.
  - **What You'll Read About:** After the enemy has been destroyed, Christ will come to rule and judge in righteousness. There will be peace everywhere, and God will gather scattered Israel.

- **2 Nephi 22:**
  - **Before You Read:** Isaiah just prophesied about the peace that will come when Israel is gathered into Christ. This chapter quotes Isaiah 12.
  - **What You'll Read About:** Covenant Israel will praise the Lord when they are gathered!

- **2 Nephi 23:**
  - **Before You Read:** Isaiah just finished a series of prophecies that outlined the entire cycle that Israel and Judah would endure, from captivity to redemption. Isaiah 13 and 14 are sometimes referred to as "the burden of Babylon", AKA the prophecy against Babylon. This chapter quotes Isaiah 13.
  - **What You'll Read About:** Babylon will be completely destroyed by their enemies with no mercy given. No one will be able to inhabit the land afterward. The Lord is merciful to His covenant people, but the wicked will perish.

- **2 Nephi 24:**
  - **Before You Read:** Isaiah had started to prophesy about the eventual destruction of Babylon in 2 Nephi 23, and this is the second part of that prophecy. This chapter quotes Isaiah 14.
  - **What You'll Read About:** The Lord will give the Israelites rest after their bondage by Babylon. Lucifer fell from heaven because of his pride and rebellion. King Ahaz dies.

- **2 Nephi 25:**
  - **Before You Read:** For the past 13 chapters, Nephi has been sharing teachings from the prophet Isaiah. In this chapter, Nephi now shares his own thoughts and testimony of the Savior.
  - **What You'll Read About:** Nephi glories in plainness and in the words of Isaiah, who prophesied for the Jews to understand. Nephi teaches that Jerusalem has been destroyed, and that the Messiah will live in Jerusalem, die, and then rise from the dead. Nephi teaches that his words will be preserved so he can persuade his posterity to believe in Christ. They will follow the Law of Moses until Christ fulfills it.

# SPIRITUAL GUIDING QUESTIONS

Question: What do these verses teach you about the importance of humility? (2 Nephi 20:15-16)

Question: What is one way that the Lord has comforted you? (2 Nephi 22:1)

Question: What does that mean to you that the Savior can be our strength and song?
(2 Nephi 22:2)

Question: What stands out to you from this description of Lucifer's intentions and fate?
(2 Nephi 24:12-16)

Question: Why is it important that we all have different teaching and learning styles? What is Nephi's style vs. Isaiah's style? Who is a current church teacher with whom you seem to connect with their style of teaching? (2 Nephi 25:1-7)

Question: Looking back since the restoration began, what are some of the biggest examples that the Lord is doing a marvelous work and a wonder? (2 Nephi 25:17)

Question: Why is it important that we talk, rejoice in, and teach of Christ? How can you improve at doing this? (2 Nephi 25:23, 26)

# 2 NEPHI 26 - 30

## *"A Marvelous Work and a Wonder"*

# BIG PICTURE

*How to feel confident fitting in this week's readings with the entire New Testament*

## General Context:

- **"I cannot read a sealed book."** In February 1828, Martin Harris brought a paper with some characters Joseph had copied off the gold plates along with the translation to Professor Charles Anthon. Initially, Anthon agreed that the translation was correct. However, when Martin mentioned *how* the characters had been obtained, Anthon rescinded his statement because he did not believe in the ministering of angels. He said that if Martin could bring him the actual plates, *he* could translate them. When Martin replied that part of the plates were sealed, and he was forbidden to bring them, Charles Anthon replied, "I cannot read a sealed book." (Read Joseph Smith-History 1:64-65.)

- **In 2 Nephi 27, Nephi prophesies about this exact experience!** In this chapter, when a learned man is told the book he wants to translate is sealed, he replies "I cannot read it." So, why is it important that Nephi includes a prophecy that will happen thousands of years in the future in a professor's office? **It shows that God works through the weak and simple.** When God wanted to bring forth the Book of Mormon and translate it into modern language, He didn't use the learned. He used Joseph Smith-- someone who would be humble enough to rely on Him.

- **This week, we get to hear from Nephi!** He is continuing his teachings that began in 2 Nephi 11. In chapters 26-30 this week, Nephi will teach more about Jesus Christ. You'll also notice that Nephi will prophesy- he is receiving and sharing unique prophecies that were not only useful for his people, but also for us in the latter days. Although we have finished Nephi's main quotations from Isaiah, you may notice that chapter 27 is filled with Nephi's interpretation of Isaiah's teachings found in Isaiah 29. He weaves in quotes from Isaiah, paraphrases, and adds his own thoughts throughout the chapter.

# Spiritual Themes:

Look for these themes as you read the chapters this week! Find examples in the scriptures, and ponder on what these themes can look like in your life.

- **The coming forth of the Book of Mormon**

- **Avoiding the strategies of the adversary**

- **Including everyone**

# People to Know:

- **Nephi**
  - Nephi is the prophet-leader to his people in the land of Nephi in the promised land. He has been working to lead his people in righteousness as they establish a new society together. He is writing on plates the teachings that are of the most spiritual importance to both his people in the future, and to us as the ultimate recipients.

# Where are We?

- **The Land of Nephi**
  - Nephi and the other righteous members of his family had separated themselves and established their new home in a place they called the land of Nephi. It was first established right before 570 B.C. The people were industrious and built up the land, including constructing a temple. Nephi makes the small plates and records his teachings here in Nephi.

# LITTLE PICTURE

*How to understand each chapter and apply principles to my life*

- **2 Nephi 26:**
  - **Before You Read:** Nephi has been writing some of his teachings to his people. In the previous chapter, he wrote about Isaiah's teachings and prophesied about the coming of the Messiah.
  - **What You'll Read About:** Nephi prophesies about Christ appearing to the Nephites, and the signs that will accompany His coming. He teaches that a few generations after Christ's coming, his people will be destroyed for their wickedness. He prophesies more about the Gentiles building up many churches and secret combinations in the last days. Christ welcomes all to partake in His salvation. Jesus gives His commandments out of love, and all are alike unto God.

- **2 Nephi 27:**
  - **Before You Read:** In the previous chapter, Nephi prophesied about the destruction of his people and the development of many churches among the Gentiles. This chapter quotes most of Isaiah 29, although it is not identical and Nephi adds some more details to Isaiah's prophecy.
  - **What You'll Read About:** There will be apostasy on the earth, until the Lord brings forth the words of the Book of Mormon. The book will be sealed and the learned will not be able to read it. God will perform miracles and the unlearned will help bring forth the Book of Mormon. The Lord will perform a marvelous work and a wonder. Those who refuse to trust in the Lord will eventually learn the doctrine.

- **2 Nephi 28:**
  - **Before You Read:** Nephi just used some more of Isaiah's prophecies to teach about the miraculous coming forth of the Book of Mormon in the last days. Nephi will now prophesy.
  - **What You'll Read About:** In the last days, many churches will be built up, but not unto the Lord. Many will live wickedly, saying God will save them anyway. Wo unto the learned, rich, and proud who feel secure. The devil will flatter and pacify people – convincing them that they already know it all and all is well.

- **2 Nephi 29:**
  - **Before You Read:** Nephi has been prophesying about the philosophies of the devil that will prevail for many in the last days.
  - **What You'll Read About:** When God brings forth the Book of Mormon, there will be many that will reject it because they already have a Bible. God sends us multiple witnesses and books to show that His word is the same, and He speaks to multiple groups of people. Hearing the words from multiple sources is a way God keeps His covenant.

- **2 Nephi 30:**
  - **Before You Read:** In the previous chapter, Nephi taught about the coming forth of the Book of Mormon.
  - **What You'll Read About:** Gentiles and Jews who believe in Christ will be numbered together; one group is not better than the other. Nephi teaches that the remnant of his people and a remnant of Jews will receive the Book of Mormon and become a delightsome people. The wicked will be destroyed, followed by a time of peace when everything will be revealed.

# SPIRITUAL GUIDING QUESTIONS

Question: What is the Lord's motivation for everything that He does? Why is this important to remember? (2 Nephi 26:24)

Question: Who is not allowed to partake in the Lord's salvation? How can remembering this help us be better at sharing the gospel? (2 Nephi 26:27-28)

Question: When is a time that you felt "unqualified" to fulfill a calling at church? What does the Lord actually look for in the people who serve? (2 Nephi 27:19-20)

Question: How do you feel about the quality of your prayers right now? How can you make them more sincere? (2 Nephi 27:25)

Question: Which of the philosophies of the adversary might be most enticing to you? How can you protect yourself from that temptation? (2 Nephi 28:5-9)

Question: How do you avoid becoming complacent with your current spiritual status, without being overwhelmed with guilt? (2 Nephi 28:24)

Question: Why did the Lord give us both the Bible and the Book of Mormon? What is one way the Book of Mormon has been a blessing to you? (2 Nephi 29:7-9)

# 2 NEPHI 31 - 33

## "This is the Way"

# BIG PICTURE

*How to feel confident fitting in this week's readings with the entire New Testament*

## General Context:

- **These are our final teachings from Nephi.** As we finish up with 2 Nephi, we have to say goodbye to our narrator up to this point. And as much as I don't want to leave Nephi's beautiful teachings, stories, and example, I always love to focus on how each writer in the scriptures chooses to end their writings. What did Nephi think was most important that he had to include? It seems like Nephi knew and expected this to be the last thing he wrote, so as you read this week, look for what Nephi made sure to emphasize before handing over the plates.

- **Speaking of the plates, let's do a quick refresher.** Nephi made two different plates: the large plates had mostly the history of the people, and the small plates had mostly spiritual teachings and commentary. Do you remember which plates we are reading a translation of? That's right, the SMALL plates of Nephi. Even though we don't have records of what Nephi wrote on the large plates during his lifetime, it's important to remember that both of these records exist and are being passed from writer to writer, starting with Nephi as their creator. The large plates will come into play soon. . .
  - Also, just to be clear, these are totally different than the "brass plates" that Lehi and his family got from Laban and carried over to the promised land. Think of the brass plates as their version of the Old Testament scriptures. This is where Nephi and Jacob had record of Isaiah's words.

- **What is the doctrine of Christ?** In these final chapters, Nephi is going to talk a lot about the "doctrine of Christ". Simply put, the doctrine of Christ is made of the steps Jesus showed us we need to take in order to return to live in His kingdom. These steps are typically separated into 5 sections:
  - **Faith in Jesus Christ**
  - **Repentance**
  - **Baptism**
  - **Receiving the gift of the Holy Ghost**
  - **Enduring to the end**

- As you read Nephi's final teachings, see if you can find which element of "the doctrine of Christ" he is focusing on in each verse.

# Spiritual Themes:

Look for these themes as you read the chapters this week! Find examples in the scriptures, and ponder on what these themes can look like in your life.

- **The doctrine of Christ**

- **Pray always**

- **The gift of the Holy Ghost**

# People to Know:

- **Nephi**
  - Nephi is the writer of this book, and has been our narrator for the entire Book of Mormon so far. He is a prophet, and was appointed leader of the Nephites, the righteous group who left the Land of First Inheritance when their wicked family members threatened Nephi's life. These chapters will be the final words we hear from Nephi.
- **Jacob**
  - Jacob is Nephi's younger brother who was born during their journeying in the wilderness. Once he moved to the land of Nephi, Jacob was ordained and consecrated to preach to the people of Nephi as a teacher and priest. Nephi recorded some teachings from Jacob in 2 Nephi. Looking ahead, the next book we'll read is Jacob- so we'll get to hear a lot more from him!

# Where are We?

- **The Land of Nephi**
  - Nephi and the other righteous members of his family had separated themselves and established their new home in a place they called the land of Nephi. It was first established right before 570 B.C. The people were industrious and built up the land, including constructing a temple. This is where Nephi is as he records his teachings.

# LITTLE PICTURE

*How to understand each chapter and apply principles to my life*

- **2 Nephi 31:**
  - **Before You Read:** Nephi has been recording the most important teachings from himself, his brother Jacob, and Isaiah throughout 2 Nephi. He now shares his final prophecies and teachings. Look for elements of the doctrine of Christ.
  - **What You'll Read About:** Nephi wants to teach plainly about the doctrine of Christ. He teaches about why Christ was baptized and received the Holy Ghost, and what that means for us as an example. Christ teaches that we must be baptized and then endure to the end. We must continue with faith and steadfastness if we want to enter the Kingdom of God.

- **2 Nephi 32:**
  - **Before You Read:** In the previous chapter, Nephi wrote about the doctrine of Christ, and the importance of steadfastly enduring to the end.
  - **What You'll Read About:** Nephi teaches that angels speak by the power of the Holy Ghost, and that we must seek and ask God to understand His words. Pray always and God will bless all you do.

- **2 Nephi 33:**
  - **Before You Read:** In the previous chapter, Nephi taught about the Holy Ghost and the importance of praying always. These are the final words that we read from Nephi.
  - **What You'll Read About:** Nephi prays that his weak words will be made strong, and glories in Jesus. He has charity for all, and asks everyone to believe in the words that he wrote about Christ. His words will be a witness at the judgment bar.

# SPIRITUAL GUIDING QUESTIONS

Question: Why was Christ baptized? What can you learn from His example? (2 Nephi 31:4-10)

Question: What does "endure to the end" look like to you? (2 Nephi 31:16)

Question: What is one way that you feast upon the words of Christ? (2 Nephi 32:3)

Question: What is a question you have in your life right now? How can you invite the
Holy Ghost to direct you? (2 Nephi 32:5)

Question: How does the adversary tempt you to skip prayers? How can you pray even more in
your life than you are right now? (2 Nephi 32:8-9)

Question: What do you think it means to consecrate your actions to the Lord? What is a promised
blessing if we pray with intention and consecrate our lives to the Lord? (2 Nephi 32:9)

Question: How does the Holy Ghost help us communicate and teach effectively,
despite our weaknesses? (2 Nephi 33:1)

# Congratulations for finishing January-March in the Book of Mormon!

Ready for more scripture study resources?

## Keep the momentum going!

Check comefollowmestudy.com or my social media channels @comefollowmestudy for more information on how to get your Book of Mormon Study Guide for April-June! Thank you for your continued support.

Got any questions or feedback? I'd love to hear from you at caliblack@comefollowmestudy.com.

Created by Cali Black, Come Follow Me Study, LLC. This material is copyrighted. It is intended for use in one household. For additional permissions, contact Cali at caliblack@comefollowmestudy.com.

This material is neither made, provided, approved, nor endorsed by Intellectual Reserve, Inc. or The Church of Jesus Christ of Latter-day Saints. Any content or opinions expressed, implied or included in or with the material are solely those of the owner and not those of Intellectual Reserve, Inc. or The Church of Jesus Christ of Latter-day Saints.

Made in the USA
Las Vegas, NV
14 January 2024

84364279R00052